A BEGINNER'S GUIDE TO
KNITTING ON A LOOM

ISELA PHELPS

Search Press

FULLY REVISED AND UPDATED EDITION OF THE BESTSELLING BOOK

A Beginner's Guide to Knitting on a Loom,
Second Edition.

A QUINTET BOOK

First published in the UK in 2016 by
Search Press Ltd.
Wellwood,
North Farm Road,
Tunbridge Wells
Kent TN2 3DR
United Kingdom

www.searchpress.com

ISBN: 978-1-78221-478-6

This book was conceived, designed
and produced by
Quintet Publishing Limited
4th Floor, Ovest House
58 West Street
Brighton,
East Sussex BN1 2RA
UK

First Edition

Senior Editor: Ruth Patrick
Editor: Katy Bevan
Designer: Steve West
Photographer: Paul Forrester
Photographic Art Director: Katy Bevan
Illustrator: Anthony Duke
Creative Director: Richard Dewing
Publisher: Gaynor Sermon

Second Edition

Project Editor: Katy Denny
Designer: Bonnie Bryan
Photographer: Lydia Evans
Art Director: Michael Charles
Publisher: Mark Searle

10 9 8 7 6 5 4 3 2 1

Manufactured in China by 1010 Printing
International Ltd.

Getty Images: Graeme Robertson 7

Contents

Equipment and Materials

Round Loom Knitting

Introduction

Sit down, grab a loom and some yarn and let's begin an adventure. You can be knitting away in a few minutes.

Loom knitting is so easy; children and adults have come to embrace it as a relaxing pastime. You may recall using a wooden spool with four small nails to make pieces of knitted cord. The miles of cord would eventually be transformed into hot pads, placemats, and coasters. Today's knitting looms are a little different than the spool of cherished memories, but they are still easy and fun to use.

Knitting looms come in various shapes and sizes: some are rectangular, some are round, and some are even heart shaped. The size of the knitting loom dictates the size of the knitted piece that it can make. However, you can attach panels together to make wider items. You can create almost anything with a knitting loom, from knitted tubes for hats or socks, to flat panels to create scarves, belts and even sweaters.

Loom knitting is an easy craft to learn; children and adults alike can learn in a few hours. Adults who have previously struggled to needle knit can make their knitting dreams come true. Crafters who thought their making days were gone can enjoy creating again with knitting looms.

This book is designed as a hands-on book, as well as a reference book for loom knitters. In the first part of the book you will find loom knitting techniques for round looms and knitting boards. The second part of the book contains a range of projects to consolidate your new skills. Further stitch patterns and resources are included at the end to extend your loom knitting adventure.

Loom on!
Isela Phelps

Knitting Without Needles

It is believed that before knitting needles and crochet hooks, there was knitting without needles. First, it occurred through the magic of finger knitting of the Native Americans.

Soon after finger knitting, people discovered they could knit on sticks rather than using their fingers. The sticks were short and upright in a row, not like knitting needles are used, but rather like finger knitting with sticks. It is believed that these knitting sticks were the predecessors to the knitting rake or peg knitting as we know it.

The earliest knitting rake found was found in Germany, dating back to around 1535. Early knitting rakes were made from different natural resources: wood, animal horns, and even ivory.

The oldest survivor of the knitting loom family is the cherished knitting spool (known also as corker, knitting nancy, and knitting noddy or French knitter), which is very closely related to the lucet. A lucet is a two-pronged device, traditionally made of wood. The yarn is wound in a figure of eight around the two prongs, thus creating a long and strong cord. Adding beads to the cords transformed a simple cord into jewellery.

Traditionally thought of as a children's toy, the knitting spool has four or six small prongs that are used to make thicker cords than those created on the lucet. The cords can be sewn together to form rugs, coasters, and placemats and like the cords created on the Lucet, adding beads can add some pizazz to a simple cord.

As you can see, knitting looms are not new to this world. They have a rich history that can trace itself back at least 400 years. Although you will be hard pressed to find an ivory knitting frame, knitting looms can still be found today in a grand array of assorted shapes and sizes that can make your mind go around in circles. Knitting looms are currently being manufactured in wood and plastic, with the choice of wooden, plastic, or metal pegs.

Spool knitting used to dramatic effect by Françoise Dupre, Knit 2 Together at the Crafts Council, London, 2005.

Knitting looms, like knitting needles, come in different sizes. Although still being standardised in the industry, there are some recurring sizes among the knitting loom vendors. Currently, the sizes are classified as large tension, regular tension, small tension, fine tension, and extra fine tension. The smaller tensions are available only with metal pins to allow for a tighter stitch.

The tensions are determined generally by the distance from the centre of one peg to the centre of the next peg. The distances currently available can be seen in the table on page 12.

Equipment
and Materials

Meet the Family

The knitting loom family can be divided it into three subdivisions: the circular looms also known as knitting looms, double-sided rake looms, and single-sided rake looms.

Round or circular knitting looms can be used to make a specific size tube by knitting on them in the round. Each round knitting loom can only create a specific size of tube. The bigger the knitting loom, the bigger the tube it can create. They are formed by a continuous row of pegs that can be a circular, oblong, octagon, square, or even heart-shaped. The base shape of the loom does not have an impact on the look of the knitted item, as long as the loom has a continuous row of pegs.

Knitting boards, also known as double-sided rake looms, are referred to throughout the book as knitting boards. Knitting boards have two parallel rows of pegs with a gap between them that allows the knitting to fall through. They are used to create double-sided items that have no wrong side. (To learn more about knitting boards see page 68.)

The single-sided rake is a knitting loom with a single row of pegs. It is used to create a flat panel with a reverse side and a right side. Both circular looms and knitting boards can be used as a single-sided rake to knit flat panels. When a loom is being used to knit a flat panel, it is said that it is being used as a knitting rake.

During my loom knitting journey, I have seen knitting looms being sold exclusively as single-sided rakes as well as in many different shapes, sizes, and colours. A piece of advice if you have the choice of purchasing a round loom or a straight knitting rake – I recommend you choose the round loom. Although they can both be used as a knitting rake, the round loom has the advantage of being more versatile as you can use it to create tubes.

Another advantage to knitting on a round loom is that with a straight knitting rake you need to hold it on your lap and look down to work, which can

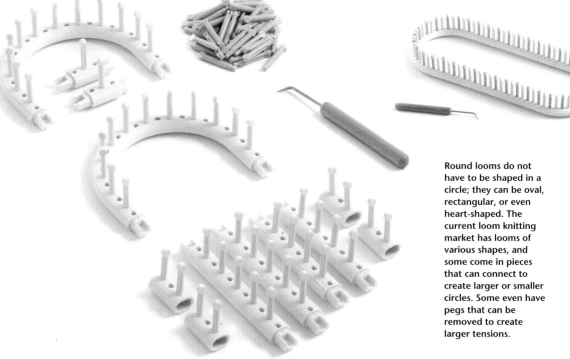

Round looms do not have to be shaped in a circle; they can be oval, rectangular, or even heart-shaped. The current loom knitting market has looms of various shapes, and some come in pieces that can connect to create larger or smaller circles. Some even have pegs that can be removed to create larger tensions.

strain your neck muscles. You could hold a rake up with one hand and wrap and knit with the other, but this puts strain on your wrists. With the round knitting looms you have the benefit of letting it stand up, perpendicular on your lap, turning it as you wrap and knit, leaving the weight of the loom and the project on your lap.

Remember, any knitting loom can be used as a knitting rake to make flat panels. Although the knitting loom may have a designated name, do not feel obligated to use it solely for that purpose. If the knitting loom is called a hat loom, it is only called a hat loom because it can make a tube that will fit a head. However, that same knitting loom can be used to make panels for a baby sweater, dishcloths, panels for a blanket, and any other garment that can be made by piecing together knitted panels.

How to choose the perfect knitting loom for you? The truth is that you are the

only one that can answer this question. You will have to take each one for a spin until you have found the perfect one that makes you feel comfortable.

On your journey, you will find that some knitting looms work better with different yarns. Different pegs let the yarn slide off more easily, or maybe you want a little bit more resistance between the yarn and the peg so the yarn doesn't come flying off the pegs. A little experience will help in your search.

Knitting looms such as the All-n-One can be used both in the round as circular looms, and as knitting boards – also known as double-sided rakes.

Double-sided rake looms have two long sides that may be held closely together to create a knitting board, or short sides may be added to create a circular loom.

Buying a Loom

It may seem daunting at first, as there are so many different looms available.
Don't panic; you will soon be adding to your extensive collection like a pro.

Knitting looms, like needles, can become expensive,
especially if you want to have each size available at
your disposal. Before purchasing one make a list of
the qualities that you are looking for – assess your
needs and see which loom can best fulfil them.

- Overall durability – will it break on the first or second
  use? If your dog happens to use it as a chew toy, will
  it survive the game?
- Wooden or plastic base – does it need any upkeep?
  Plastic is low maintenance but wood can last longer
- Tension of the loom – will it allow you to knit with the
  yarns you use the most?
- Type of peg – is a smooth peg what you are looking
  for? Or do you want a bit of resistance? If you happen
  to break one, can a peg/pin be replaced?
- Do the pegs have grooves to facilitate picking up
  the yarn loops?
- Do the pegs have knobs at the top to prevent
  the yarn from accidentally popping off?

Remember, your knitting looms are your main tools
to create your knits; finding the right one(s) will take
a little time and research.

Loom Gauge Table

Yarn Recommended	1 SUPER FINE	2 FINE	3 LIGHT	4 MEDIUM	5 BULKY	6 SUPER BULKY
Distance from centre of pin to centre of pin in centimetres	0.4	0.6	1	1.2	1.5	2
Loom Gauge	Extra Fine Gauge	Fine Gauge	Small Gauge	Regular Gauge	Large Gauge	Extra Large Gauge

Quick Reference

Large Gauge Knitting Looms
- Distance from centre of peg to centre of peg: 1.5cm (½in) or more
- **Available in:** wood and plastic, with nylon, plastic, wood, and metal pegs
- **Yarn:** Bulky weight yarns or two strands of medium weight yarns
- **Knits:** Bulky weight knits and knits that will be felted
- **Loom Tension:** Approximately 1½–2 stitches per 2.5cm (1in)
- Compared to needle knitting stitch tension: size 9mm (⅓in)

Regular Gauge Knitting Looms
- Distance from centre of peg to centre of peg: 1.2cm (½in)
- **Available in:** wood and plastic, with nylon, plastic, wood, and metal pegs
- **Yarn:** Chunky weight yarns or two strands of DK weight yarn

- **Knits:** Medium weight knits
- **Tension:** Approximately 3–3½ stitches per 2.5cm (1in)
- Compared to needle knitting stitch tension: size 6mm (¼in)

Small Gauge Knitting Looms
- Distance from centre of peg to centre of peg: 1cm (⅜in)
- **Available in:** wood and plastic, with nylon, plastic, wood and metal pegs
- **Yarn:** Aran weight/medium weight yarn
- **Knits:** Medium/light weight knits
- **Tension:** Approximately 3½–4 stitches per 2.5cm (1in)
- Compared to needle knitting stitch tension: size 4.5–5mm (³⁄₁₆in)

Fine Gauge Knitting Looms
- Distance from centre of peg to centre of peg: 6mm (¼in)

- **Available in:** wood with metal pegs (or pins)
- **Yarn:** DK weight
- **Knits:** Light weight knits
- **Tension:** Approximately 4–5 stitches per 2.5cm (1in)
- Compared to needle knitting stitch tension: size 3.75–4mm (⅛in)

Extra Fine Gauge Knitting Looms
- Distance from centre of peg to centre of peg: 4mm (⅛in)
- **Available in:** wood with metal pegs (or pins)
- **Yarn:** 4-ply weight/sock weight
- **Knits:** Light weight knits
- **Tension:** Approximately 7–8 stitches per 2.5cm (1in)
- Compared to needle knitting stitch tension: size 2.25–2.75mm (¹⁄₁₆in)

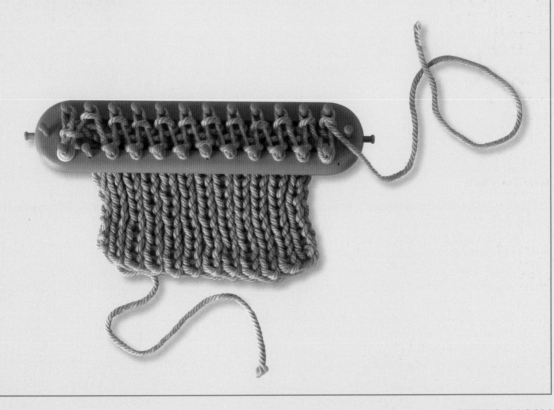

Essential Tools for Your Loomy Bag

The journey is about to begin and like any journey, we need to gather our equipment and gear up to make the journey easier and more enjoyable.

A knitting tool or pick is the most essential gadget for the loom knitter – you can never have enough of them. Have a few of them on hand, or if you are paranoid like me, you will have a drawer full, as they are sneaky and tend to hide when you need them the most.

The purpose of the knitting tool is to facilitate knitting on the loom. The tool allows you to lift the yarn up and over the peg, creating a stitch. A knitting tool is similar to a dental pick or nut pick, generally made out of metal, with a wooden or plastic handle. The end is bent at an angle to allow the lifting of the stitches. Knitting tools come with different ends: some sharp for use when knitting on very small pegs with thin yarns, some more blunt for use with bigger pegs and thicker yarns. If you happen to lose all your knitting tools, you can also use a small crochet hook, nut pick, or even an orange peeler.

A yarn guide/aid is a thin plastic tube. It facilitates wrapping the yarn around the pegs and helps keep an even tension in your wrapping. Some knitting loom vendors carry them as part of their line; if you are unable to find one, you can easily make one (see the box below).

Scissors/yarn cutters are invaluable. Some yarns are easy to break with your hands; however, you will find that many synthetic yarns and cottons are almost impossible to break. Carrying small scissors in your knitting bag is always advisable. If travelling by plane, I recommend obtaining a yarn/thread cutter that you can take along with you in your carry-on luggage.

A row counter is a nifty item to have in your knitter's bag. It comes in handy… as long as you don't forget to change the setting. Row counters come in various shapes: cylindrical, square and circular. There are two types of cylindrical shaped row counter. One of them has an opening that is usually used to insert a knitting needle through; in our case it can be fitted over the knitting tool. The second one has a small ring attached to one of the sides that allows you to put it over a peg and keep it at the base of the knitting loom. The square and circular types are mechanical in that you only need to push a button to increase the numbers.

Although all of them help in keeping track of rows, you have to remember to reset them at the beginning of each row.

How to make a Yarn Guide:

1 Find a plain-style ballpoint pen with a hollow centre.
2 Take out the ink cartridge inside.
3 Cut the tip off the barrel.
4 Sand down any rough spots with an emery board.
5 It is now ready to use. Pass the starting tail of the yarn through and wrap around the pegs with the aid of your new Yarn Guide!

No pens around? No problem. Get a thick drinking straw. Cut it so you have a piece that is about 12.5cm (5in) long. Thread your yarn through it and you are ready to start wrapping your yarn around the pegs.

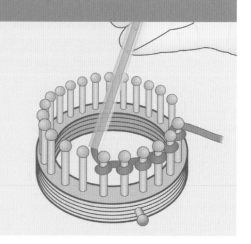

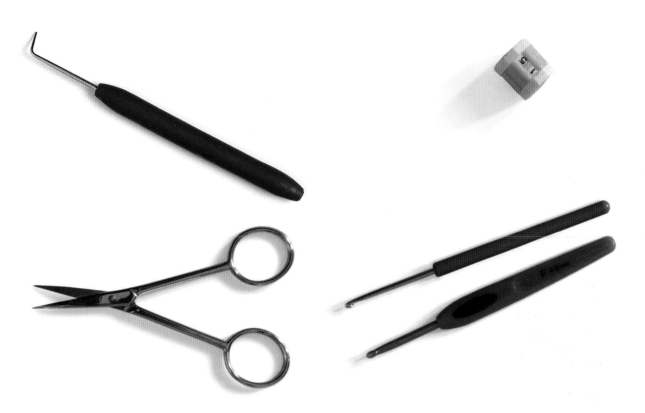

Crochet hooks are very useful – in fact essential for certain cast on and cast off methods. Crochet knowledge is not necessary to loom knit, unless you want to crochet an edging around your knits. Crochet hooks come in handy when picking up a dropped stitch or when casting off a flat panel from the knitting loom. It is preferable to have the size of crochet hook called for on the yarn label, but in general, carrying a medium size hook in your accessories bag will suffice.

A stitch tension guide allows you to determine exactly the number of stitches and rows per inch in your work. It is a flat piece of metal or plastic with ruler markings on the sides. In the centre there is a small L-shaped window that allows you to check the rows and stitches per inch of the knitted piece. If you don't have one, you could make one out of stiff card.

To check the tension, block the knitted piece lightly, place it on a flat surface then place the stitch guide on top of it. Line the bottom cut-out window opening with one row of the knitted piece. Line one of the columns of stitches to the side

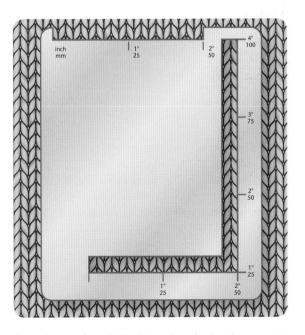

(see picture above). To determine the tension, count the stitches per 2.5cm (1in) in the window opening. Count also the rows per 2.5cm (1in). Make sure to count quarter and half stitches.

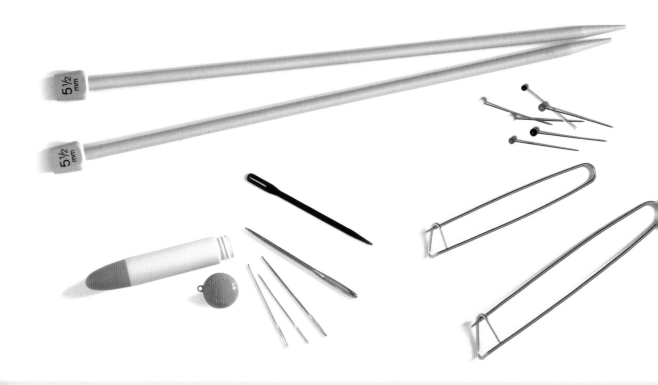

Single-pointed knitting needles. Wait! Don't run, you won't be using them to knit. There, you can relax. The needles are only going to be used as stitch holders for grafting the toes of socks. I would recommend obtaining a pair of 5mm (US size 8) and a pair of 2.75mm (US size 2). The 5mm can be used with the large and regular tension looms, while the 2.75mm can be used with the smaller tensions.

Tapestry needles are used for seaming the sides of a knitted garment, for gathering and closing the ends of hats, and for weaving in the ends on the knitted garment. Tapestry needles come in plastic and metal, and they have a larger eye than regular sewing needles. The plastic needles are flexible and allow you to bend them, while the metal needles are smoother and won't snag the knitted item. Both styles of needles have blunt ends that prevent the splitting of the yarn. As with crochet hooks, the needles come in different sizes, and the eye opening can fit certain thicknesses of yarns; it is advisable to have a collection of needles that differ in the size of the eye opening.

Pins have uses everywhere in the knitting world; they can turn a curled piece of stocking into a nice straight sleeve and are essential tools in the finishing of knitted pieces. The straight pins with coloured heads are perfect to use when seaming two sides together. Large T-pins make blocking a knitted garment a breeze. These pins can be found at any yarn shop. Do not use any other household pin as it may rust and leave rust spots on your knits.

Stitch holders look like oversized safety pins, except they have a blunt end. They are useful for holding live stitches that will be worked on later in the project, like for a neckline, or a tricky bit of shaping. They come in different sizes and it is advisable to have an array of sizes in your knitting bag. Small coil-less safety pins also come in handy when holding only a few stitches or marking the right or reverse side of the knitted item.

Stitch markers are small rings that can be used to mark the pegs where certain stitches or other special treatment needs to be made on the knitted item. Usually, the stitch markers are used on needles, however, since they are small rings, they fit perfectly over the pegs on a knitting loom and they sit at the base of the loom to remind the loomer that the peg has a stitch that requires special treatment.

Split ring stitch markers are very helpful in marking a stitch itself rather than the peg. The open split rings are removable by simply opening the ring and sliding it off the stitch. They come in various shapes, sizes, and colours. Having a variety of different colours is recommended.

A measuring tape and ruler is a loom knitter's best friend; no knitting bag should be without at least one. When choosing a good measuring tape, choose material that won't distort easily. Discard any measuring tape at the first sign of wear, even if it's your favourite. A distorted measuring tape can mean disaster to your knitted garment as it won't measure accurately. A small plastic ruler is also advisable to have on hand.

Cable needles come in different shapes and sizes. They are available in plastic and metal. Usually, one package contains three different sizes; choose the size that best works with the yarn in the project.

Until very recently, loom knitters were not able to create cables on a knitting loom, the non-elasticity of the stitches as set on the knitting loom making it difficult. However, this has changed. We are now able to create cables and thus we have added the use of cable needles to our extensive gadget repertoire!

A calculator. Yes, you read it right, we will still be doing maths. I know you thought maths was long gone with school, but maths has come to haunt you again and it wants to be your best friend. No worries though, you can cheat this time and use a calculator. A calculator comes very handy when calculating tension or even adding a few pegs to the count in the pattern.

Other Noteworthy Gear for the Journey

Sticky Notes
Stickies are a great way to mark the row on the paper pattern you are knitting from. After knitting each row, move the sticky note down the page. There are two schools of thought about sticky notes:

1 Cover the previous knitted row and expose the rows to come.
2 Cover the future rows and only expose the rows worked on.

It is up to you to decide which method works best for you.

Notebook
A place to jot down ideas about the patterns, comments about yarns, and other loomy gems.

Ball Winder
This little gadget allows you to wind your yarn into an easy-to-use centre pull ball.

Two styles are available, manual and electric, but you can always make balls the old-fashioned way with your hands.

Yarn Swift
A yarn swift is usually used in conjunction with the ball winder. It resembles the inside of an umbrella. It holds a hank of yarn and it unwinds it. When used along with the ball winder, the yarn swift unwinds the hank of yarn and the ball winder winds it into a ball. If you don't have one of these, persuade a friend to sit still with their arms outstretched while you wind your ball, or, failing that, use the back of a chair.

Nail File/Emery Board
Is your yarn catching on the pegs? Some knitting looms have small burrs on the pegs that may snag the yarn. Use the emery

board to sand down the small burrs and you have smooth looming ahead!

Knitting Bag
You need a bag that is big enough to hold your project and your knitting loom, sturdy enough to carry the weight of the knitting loom, with a comfortable handle to hold or carry around. It should have a wide opening to take out and put in all your loom knitting essentials. It should have lots of pockets to put in all the gadgets and notions and even a small snack for the reward moments. If possible, it should be waterproof so if it happens to rain, your knitting is safe. Closures should be either zips or buttons; say no to Velcro® – this will snag your yarn and can even destroy your knitted item if caught.

Yarn 101: A Quick Refresher on Yarn

One of the perks of any fibre art is the luxurious yarn 'needed' for the projects. The market is full of luscious yarns, varying in colour, texture, and fibre content.

Consider this a crash course on yarn. Before going all out and purchasing 10 skeins of that pretty yarn you fell in love with, let's take a small trip to the yarn shop and get personal with the yarns.

Hold them close to your skin; the neck or the inside of your forearm are good places to see how your skin reacts to their fibre properties. Check the colour in different lighting: move around the yarn store to see the effect that different lighting has on the yarn. If possible, ask if you can see it outside under real light. Pull at it to check its elasticity; some yarns have more elasticity than others and this can affect the overall look of the project.

Check the yarn label for important fibre-related data. The label band contains essential information, such as fibre content, colour, dye lot (if any), washing instructions, and yardage. Keep the yarn labels of any project until you have completed the project. Recently, a friend of mine moved to a different state in the US. At the time she was knitting a beautiful Fair Isle scarf and she ran out of one of the colours. Fortunately, she had saved the label and was able to match the exact dye lot at a different yarn store in her new location. Moral of the story: keep your yarn labels.

Label Close-up

1 Brand name
2 Yarn name
3 Fibre content

4 Fibre company
5 Yarn weight
6 Yardage

7 Care instructions
8 Tension indicator
(needle knitting related)

 R O W A N

 handknit cotton

3 100% COTTON 100%
BAUMWOLLE 100% COTTON

4
Rowan Yarns
Holmfirth England
Z04800

5 50g

In accordance with
B.S. 984

6
Approx length 85m
(93 yds)
www.knitrowan.com

7

 Machine wash

 Do not bleach

 Warm Iron

 Dry cleanable in all solvents

 Do not tumble dry. Dry flat out of direct sunlight.

8
19–20 sts

10cm/4in · 28 rows

10cm/4in

8–7 mm · 4–4½ mm

6–7 US

CARE INSTRUCTIONS

Dry clean or hand wash in soapflakes; do not soak; cool rinse; do not wring; short spin; do no leave wet; reshape and dry flat away from direct sunlight; use damp pressing cloth.

Yarns come wound in different shapes: cones, skeins, hanks, and balls. A cone has a cardboard centre with yarn wound around it. Its starting tail is on the outside of the cone. A ball is ready to use and, usually, has a starting tail in the centre core. Reach your hand inside, and pull out the centre. If lucky, you will find the starting tail right away. Once you start loom knitting, do not stop until you have finished knitting all the yarn you took out from the centre, or make sure to wind it loosely around the outside of the ball. A hank is a loosely wound coil of yarn, held together by a string at two sides of the coil. A skein is the hank twisted into a manageable shape, and you will need to wind it into a ball.

Yarns are divided into two groups: natural fibres, and synthetic fibres. Under natural yarns, there are two subdivisions: those that are protein based and those that are cellulose based.

Protein-based fibres are the most well known and include wool, angora, cashmere, mohair, and alpaca. Protein fibres such as wool are popular among loom knitters for their warm, elastic, and durable characteristics. Wool is known as a good all-year-round fibre.

Cellulose-based fibres are those made from plants, and cotton is the most widely known. Renowned for its cooling properties, cotton is often used for summer garments as it absorbs moisture and dries quickly, although it does not have the elasticity of wool. Another natural fibre, silk is known for its smoothness and softness. To provide elasticity or warmth, yarn manufacturers often mix these natural yarns with other fibres.

Synthetic fibres have opened the door to a fun world of novelty yarns: think funky, sparkly, nobbly textures. Synthetic yarns have the great advantage of being machine washable, making them a good choice for children's loom knits. However, synthetics are hot and are not absorbent so can leave the wearer feeling like they just came out of a steam room session. Manufacturers have combined synthetics with other fibres to achieve certain qualities that other fibres may lack.

Yarn Weights

Yarns come in different thicknesses, known as weights. The thicker the yarn, the bigger the stitches. Yarn weights range from fine to bulky. The finer the yarn, the closer the pegs need to be on the knitting loom.

The table below gives a standard reference guide for yarn and the use of it on knitting looms. Choosing the right yarn for the project can be a little bit daunting when starting out.

Variegated colour yarns work best with simple stocking or other simple stitches that allow the beauty of the colours to show. Textured stitches will be hard to see through the colour changes.

Solid colour yarns are great for cables or any other stitch patterns. Cables show better with light colour yarns.

Novelty yarns look best worked in simple stocking or garter stitch to show off the special characteristics of the yarn; anything more complex won't show.

Once you have chosen the yarn for your project, knit up a small swatch and wash it a couple of times. Check for the following: colourfastness, pilling, drape, shrinkage, and most importantly does it show the stitch pattern as you imagined it?

Yarn weight symbol	**1** SUPER FINE	**2** FINE	**3** LIGHT	**4** MEDIUM	**5** BULKY	**6** SUPER BULKY
Types of yarn	2-ply, Fingering, Sock Weight	4-ply	DK	Aran	Chunky	Bulky
Knit tension in stocking stitch per 2.5 cm	7–8	5–6	4–5	3–4	2–3	1.5–2
Recommended knitting loom tension	Extra Fine Tension	Fine Tension	Small Tension	Regular Tension	Regular/ Large Tension	Large Tension

Loom Knitting Felts

A decade or so ago, I acquired a gorgeous cashmere sweater. It was my favourite sweater to wear. Then, the dreaded day came when I had to wash it.

Although I read the instructions on the label, my inexperience won and I threw it in the laundry with all my other clothes. Then, the most devastating thing occurred – my sweater came out big enough to fit a newborn baby. I quickly assumed that it was the washer that had caused the shrinkage in my lovely sweater. Fast forwards a few years and now I am throwing things in the washer to make them smaller on purpose.

Since the death of that sweater, I have learned that it was not the washer that killed it, but a combination of different factors. The agitation in the washer, the changes in water temperature, and the detergent all combined to open the scales of the fibre, and as the scales opened, they interlocked with each other forming a thick, impermeable fabric. The sturdy fabric created by felting (also known as 'fulling') is perfect for many items like bags and slippers.

Yarns for Felting

In order to felt successfully, the item needs to be knitted loosely with non-super-wash wool, or yarns that have a high natural fibre content like mohair, llama, angora, or alpaca.

Light coloured yarns such as white and off-white take longer to felt than dark coloured yarns and, at times, they do not felt. The reason for light coloured yarns felting at a slower rate is because they have been through a bleaching process that has damaged the fibre scales. Before felting with any light coloured yarns, make sure to knit a test sample swatch.

The easiest way to find out the properties of the yarn is by studying its label. Common telltales that the yarn may felt are instructions to wash by hand with cold water, and fibre content. If the yarn is labelled Superwash – stop, do not start your project with it. Superwash yarn has been treated to be machine washable and its felting capabilities have been greatly diminished.

Items to be felted need to be knitted at a very loose tension; for this reason, the large or extra large tension knitting looms are preferred.

You are probably ready to cast on your knitting loom – but let's wait for a bit. Although we will be purposely shrinking our knitted fabric, making a swatch can tell us many things about our yarn. Certain yarns tend to felt very quickly, while others may take up to four cycles, yet others may not even show any tendency to felt at all.

Quick Yarn Felting Test

Cut about 2m (2yd) of yarn. Fill a small bowl with warm water and a drop of dishwashing soap. Immerse the yarn and roll it around your palms; keep rolling it for about 5 minutes. Take it out and inspect it – pull at it. If the yarn has clumped together and does not come apart, then the yarn has felting capabilities.

Felting Swatches

Before embarking on your felting adventure, you need to make a swatch – no really, you do.

One of these will allow you to see how the yarn behaves when you wash it. Knit a small sample. I prefer to knit a square about 25 x 25cm (10 x 10in), a sample size that can always be used as a coaster or as a pocket inside a bag.

Knit your sample swatch using exactly the same yarn and stitch you plan to use for your project. If using colour combinations, knit the sample with the same colour combinations. Some yarns, even same brand yarns, do not felt at the same rate for different colours. Before throwing it in the washer, let's mark it up to learn how much shrinkage to expect. Use cotton thread in a contrasting colour (don't use the same colour as you may not be able to see it after it is felted) to mark 10cm (4in) of stitches, and 10cm (4in) of rows. Felt your sample swatch and allow it to air

dry. Measure your felted tension by finding the thread markers and measuring. If you have the correct tension, you may go forth and begin your project. If the desired tension was not achieved, try with a different yarn.

Let's Shrink It

It has been said that felting knitted items is an art more than a science. You come across it by inspiration. Each felted item is unique. Enjoy the adventure!

What You Need

These are the main items you will need apart from your yarn and loom.

Zipped Pillowcase

This splendid item will allow the knitted item to be kept separate in the washer. It keeps all the fibre away from the washer's drain. Using the zipped pillowcase protects the knitted item from distorting inside the washer as it prevents it from becoming tangled.

Agitator Helpers

Take a trip to the local charity shop and pick up a pair of light coloured jeans for light felted knits and a pair of dark coloured jeans for dark knits. Try not to use towels as agitator helpers as they may shed lint on your felted item and you'll end up with unwanted speckles.

Soap

No-rinse wool soap or shampoo will allow the scales of the wool fibres to soften during the wash. I like to use Eucalan Wool Wash as it has a hint of lavender so it subdues the wet, woolly smell.

Felting It

1 Place the knitted item inside the zipped pillowcase. Close the zip.
2 Set the washer to the smallest load setting and hottest wash.
3 Add a teaspoon of shampoo or no-rinse wool soap. Throw in the agitator helpers and the zipped pillow case. Close the door and start the washer.
4 Check the process after five minutes. Stop the washer. Reach in and take out the zipped pillowcase. If the item is the desired size, take it out. If the item is not the desired size, throw it back in the zipped pillowcase and re-start the washer. Check again in a few minutes. If possible do not let the washer go into the spin cycle as it can create creases in your project. If you have no choice, select the slowest spin speed.
5 When item has reached the desired size, remove it from zipped pillowcase and rinse it out if you used shampoo. Rinse it in the same water temperature as in the washer. If you used no-rinse wool soap you do not need to rinse.
6 Place the item between two towels and squeeze out as much water as possible.

Pull It into Shape

Your item is felted, your masterpiece is almost done; all it needs is a place to take its desired shape. If possible, find a suitable shape for your masterpiece to mold itself on. Find a box for bags or make one out of two pieces of cardboard and use plastic bags to cover them and to use as filler for the inside. Other items like slippers can be filled with plastic bags for the toe and a piece of cardboard for the sole (cover the cardboard with plastic bags). Go ahead and pull and tug your felted item into shape. If one of the corners is not looking the way you imagined, pull it into shape.

Allow your felted item to air dry completely; you can take the shape helpers out after 12 hours to speed up the drying process inside the item. Do not put the felted item in the dryer as this can shrink your item further.

Troubleshooting

How do I know when it is ready?

Look closely at your fabric; do you like the look of it? Some loom knitters like their knitted items to have stitch definition. If you like the way it looks, it is ready. If the item is not the desired size, then it is not ready.

It is too big

If your item is too big, throw it back in the washer for a few more minutes/cycles. Keep a close watch and keep washing it until it reaches the desired size.

It is too small

Don't despair, all is not lost. Wet the item completely and pull it to the desired dimensions. If, after pulling and tugging, the desired sized is not achieved, try looking for the silver lining. Cut the felted piece into other usable items: coasters, glasses case, small coin bag, or even a small rug.

It is out of shape

No, it doesn't need to go on the treadmill; it is not that kind of out of shape. If the item is crooked, try stretching it into the desired shape, pin it down and allow it to air dry pinned down.

Caring for your felted knits

Handwash felted knits in warm water. Do not over-rub; immerse in the water and gently wash.

Fuzzy problems

If the item has become fuzzy, use a razor to trim out the excess fuzz.

Stretch problems

Handles are particularly prone to becoming elongated with prolonged use, especially on bags which may need to hold heavier items. Sew a piece of grosgrain ribbon to the underside. Use the same type of ribbon to stabilise bag openings.

Round Loom Knitting

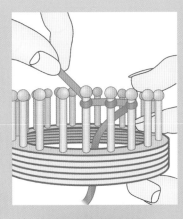

Building Blocks

Let's take our knitting loom for a little test ride. If this is your first time loom knitting, grab a skein of yarn, preferably a plain colour with some wool content.

Casting On

The foundation row for our loom knits is called the cast-on row. There are various cast-on methods, but we will only address the most basic one in this section. Every cast-on method starts with a first stitch known as a slip knot. Why a slip knot, you may ask? A slip knot allows you to make the loop bigger or smaller by pulling on the loop. It can also untie fairly easily.

Slip Knot

1 Leaving a 12.5cm (5in) beginning tail, form a circle with the working yarn.

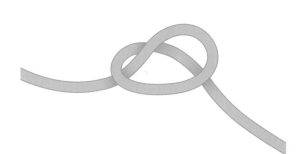

2 Hold the circle where the yarn crosses and flip it over so the loop is on top of the working yarn that comes from the skein.

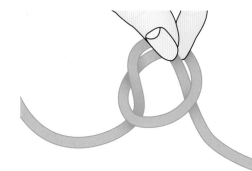

3 Reach through the circle, and grab the yarn coming from the skein.

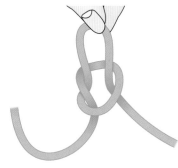

4 Pull the working yarn loop through the circle, while also pulling gently on the short end of the yarn tail end, thus tightening the noose on the knot. Slip knot completed.

Long Tail Cast On

This is known as the Long Tail Cast On because you use the tail of the yarn and the working yarn to create the cast on. This term is also used in needle knitting. It creates a flexible cast on.

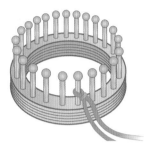

1 Make a slip knot, leaving a tail that is about four times as long as the width of your project. Place the slip knot on a peg. The slip knot will become your first stitch.

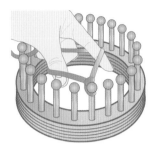

2 Position your left hand palm down: wrap the working yarn around your index finger and the tail over your thumb. Hold both yarn ends with the remaining three fingers.

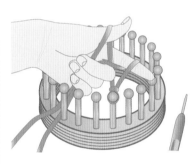

3 Flip your hand towards the left until your palm faces up. The hand is now in a slingshot position.

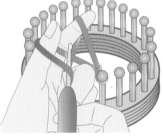

4 Guide a crochet hook by the palm side of the thumb under the yarn strand, then guide it over to the yarn strand on the index finger, hook the yarn strand on the index finger, and guide it down through the loop on your thumb.

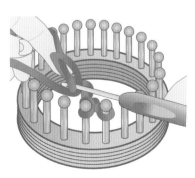

5 Place the loop on the adjacent empty peg. Remove your thumb from its loop and gently tug on the yarn tail to tighten the new stitch that you created. Repeat steps 3–5 until you have the number of stitches called for in the pattern.

No crochet hook?

There is a method of using the long tail cast on without a crochet hook but it is slightly more complicated.

1 With the slip knot on your first peg, grab the tail yarn and E-Wrap (see page 30) the peg to the left. The peg now has two loops. Knit over so only one loop remains.

2 Grab yarn coming from the skein and E-Wrap the next empty peg.

3 Grab the tail yarn and place it above the E-Wrap completed in step 2. Lift the bottom loop over and off the peg (the peg should remain wrapped with the tail).

4 Repeat steps 2 and 3 with the remaining pegs.

TIPS

You may find it more comfortable to place the loom on your lap or a table to work the cast on.

When making your slip knot, it is better to overestimate and make the tail too long rather than too short.

The E-Wrap Cast On

This cast on is called the E-Wrap because if you look at it from an aerial view it resembles a cursive 'e'. It is the easiest method to learn.

Use the E-Wrap Cast-On method when the first row needs to be picked up for a brim or seam or the cast-on row needs to be extremely flexible.

1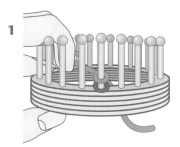

Place a stitch marker on any of the pegs on the knitting loom. The peg with the stitch marker will be your starting peg. Make a slip knot, and place it on the peg with the stitch marker.

2 Holding the knitting loom in front of you with the working yarn in your left hand, work around the loom in a clockwise direction thus: * Pull the working yarn towards the inside of the loom, wrap anticlockwise around the peg directly to the left. * Repeat from * to * with each of the pegs. Continue wrapping each peg in an anticlockwise direction, until you complete one round (each peg should have 1 loop). Notice how the yarn crosses over itself on the inside of the knitting loom.

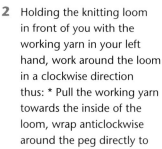

3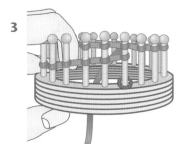

Wrap each peg a second time in the same way as step 2. Each peg should have 2 loops on it. Hold the working yarn in place so the wraps do not unravel.

4 With the knitting tool/pick, insert the tip of the tool into the bottommost loop on the last peg wrapped. Lift the loop up and off the peg and allow the loop to fall towards the inside of the knitting loom. The process of lifting the loops off the pegs is known as knitting over, abbreviated as KO. Go to the peg directly to the left and repeat the knitting over. Repeat all around the loom until each peg has only one wrap. Steps 1–4 constitute the casting on set-up. The knitting loom is now ready.

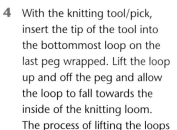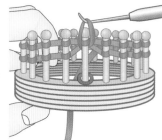

Using the anchor peg

Some loom knitters prefer to use the anchor peg on their knitting loom to anchor their slip knot. This is a small peg that appears at the side of some looms. If there isn't one you can use a thumbtack to secure the slip knot. To use the anchor peg when casting on, make a slip knot leaving a 12.5cm (5in) tail. Place the slip knot on the anchor peg on the side of your knitting loom. Perform steps 2–4 as before then remove the slip knot from the anchor peg.

Using the Loom

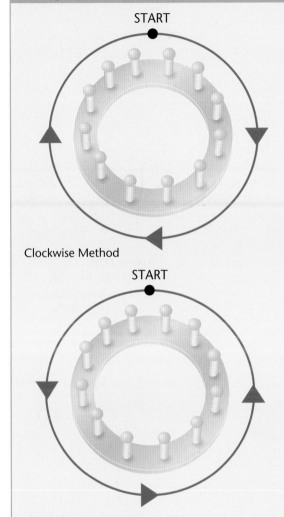

Clockwise Method

Anticlockwise Method

In loom knitting there are two ways to work. In needle knitting, you have the continental and English methods – in loom knitting we have the clockwise and anticlockwise methods.

In the clockwise method, you will find yourself working around your knitting loom in a clockwise direction. Begin knitting on the left side of the starting peg.

In the anticlockwise method, you will find yourself working around the knitting loom in an anticlockwise direction. You will begin knitting on the peg to the right of your starting peg.

Both of the methods achieve the same goal. Choose the one that feels most comfortable to you. When working on the knitting loom, it doesn't matter which way you hold the knitting loom, with pegs facing you, or opposite you, or with the loom upside down. The knitting still looks the same.

A note of warning: when reading patterns, find out in which direction the pattern is worked. If you read the pattern in the wrong direction, you will end up with a mirror image of the design. The designs in this book are worked in a clockwise direction around the knitting loom.

Loom Anatomy

There are some basic parts to the loom that you will become increasingly familiar with. This is a circular loom, but the elements are the same whether it is rake, board or round.

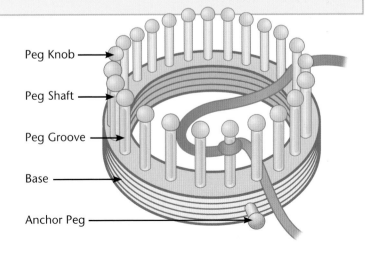

Peg Knob

Peg Shaft

Peg Groove

Base

Anchor Peg

First Stitches

Your foundation row is set up. Now we need to learn a few basic stitches to begin knitting on our loom. Luckily the E-Wrap method we used for the cast on can also be used to create stitches on the knitting loom.

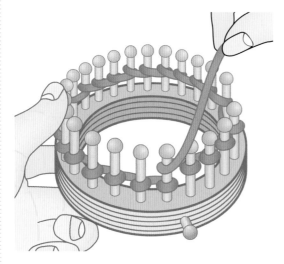

Single Stitch (ss)

To create the Single Stitch, just E-Wrap around the peg, and knit over by lifting the bottom loop up and off the peg. The Single Stitch creates what is known as a Twisted Knit Stitch.

Wrapping the entire loom and then knitting over may be quicker, but can create a ladder effect between the first and last peg knitted. In addition, since you are knitting in the round, if you wrap all the pegs then knit them over, your item will have a tendency to twist and you will see your vertical lines of stitches spiral around the item. Instead, it is better to E-Wrap and knit over one peg at a time.

WRAPPING THE LOOM

Although it is easier to wrap the entire loom two times with the E-Wrap method, then lift the bottom loop on all the pegs, I would advise you to do otherwise.

Advantages in knitting one peg at a time:
1 It will help eliminate the laddering effect between the first and last peg.
2 It will help in lessening the spiral effect of the stitches around the item.
3 Less chance of the dreaded 'boing' effect (see below)!
4 The stitches won't get too tight.

GLOSSARY

Boing Effect The sudden unravelling of your stitches is known as the 'boing' effect! By knitting over on the last peg wrapped first, you secure the stitches on the knitting loom, preventing them from unravelling.

The Double Stitch (ds)

This is also known as the one-over-two. The knitting loom needs to be prepared with three loops on each peg, and then the bottommost loop on the peg is lifted over and off the peg. This produces a tighter stitch than the single stitch. It also resembles the Twisted Knit Stitch.

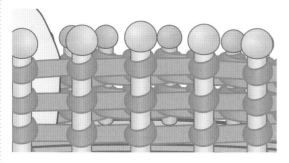

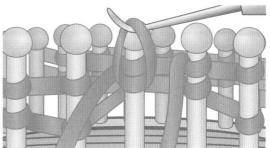

1 Cast on your knitting loom. E-wrap all around the knitting loom two more times. There should be three loops on each peg.

2 Knit over by picking the bottommost strand off the peg (two loops remain). Repeat this all around the loom until you reach the last peg.

The Half Stitch (hs)

The Half Stitch is thus named as you have to E-Wrap around the loom four times, then knit two loops over two loops. It produces a thicker stitch than the double stitch. As with the Single Stitch, and the Double Stitch, the knitting will resemble the Twisted Knit Stitch. If you are knitting with a thin yarn on a large tension knitting loom, this stitch is ideal.

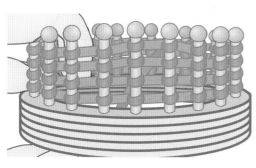

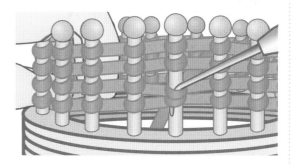

1 Cast on your knitting loom. E-wrap all around the knitting loom three more times. Each peg has four loops.

2 Knit over by lifting the lower two strands over the top two strands and off the peg. Repeat all around the knitting loom. Two loops remain on each peg.

Chunky Braid Stitch (cbs)

This stitch resembles a knitted braid. It is also known as the Three-Over-One Stitch, or Braid Stitch. It produces a thick, non-stretchy fabric with a very tight stitch. If you are knitting with a thin yarn, you may want to use this stitch throughout your project to get a firm tension.

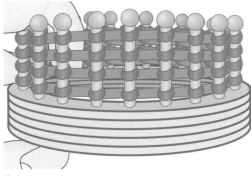

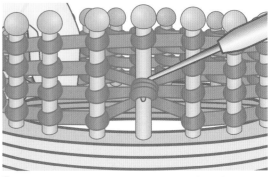

1 Cast on your knitting loom. E-wrap all around the knitting loom three more times. Each peg should now have four loops.

2 Knit over by lifting the bottommost three loops over the top loop and off the peg. Repeat the knitting over process all round the loom. One loop remains on each peg.

The above stitches are variations of stitches you can accomplish with the E-Wrap method. They all produce a Twisted Stocking-Stitch fabric.

Many of the variations of the E-Wrap require you to wrap your entire loom first then knit over. A tightness problem arises when knitting in this form. Although you may not notice it right away, if you wrap the yarn too tight around the pegs, your future rows in the piece will become very tight, making it almost impossible to knit over.

If the yarn is wrapped too tight, try this:
- Use a yarn guide to wrap your yarn around the pegs. The yarn guide will help maintain a loose and even tension all around the loom.
- Before E-Wrapping all around the loom, pull sufficient yarn from the ball to E-Wrap one entire row. Having the yarn loosely next to you will help in maintaining a loose tension on your wrapping.
- When knitting over, try pulling the loop away from the peg first, then lifting it over the peg.

If the loops become too loose, try this:
- Use a yarn guide to wrap the yarn around the pegs. The yarn guide will help in keeping an even tension around the loom.
- When knitting over, clear the loop just enough to go over the ball on the peg.

Finishing

Now that we know some stitches, let's cover some basic removals. Removing an item off the knitting loom is known as casting off, or binding off.

Gather Cast Off

The gather removal method allows you to finish a tube into a gathered end, perfect for finishing hats. Knit the tube until you have reached the desired length. If you are using any of the E-Wrap stitch variations on pages 32–4, knit over until 1 loop is left on each peg.

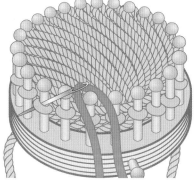

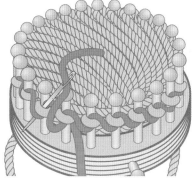

1 Cut the working yarn leaving about a 60cm (24in) tail. Thread the yarn onto a tapestry needle (contrast colour used in diagrams for clarity).

2 Starting at peg 1, insert the needle from below the loop and pull the yarn through. Moving clockwise, insert the needle into the loop on the adjacent peg from top to bottom, and repeat around the loom. Once you reach the last peg, insert the needle through the first loop one more time to avoid having a gap between the first and last loops.

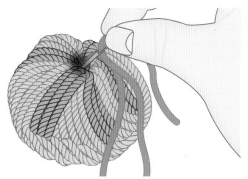

3 Remove the loops from the pegs. Gently pull on the beginning and end tails of the gathering yarn. Continue pulling on the tail ends until the top of the item has been cinched closed.

4 Poke the needle through the hole at the centre top of the hat. If the hole is big, use the needle to sew it closed. Grab the yarn tail coming from the knitting of the hat. Tie the three strands (two ends from the gathering yarn and one from the hat) together. Make a square knot and weave in the ends (see page 37).

Basic Cast Off

This creates a firm, crochet-like edge. It is a good overall cast-off method for flat panels.

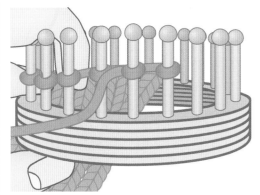

1 Knit pegs 1 and 2.

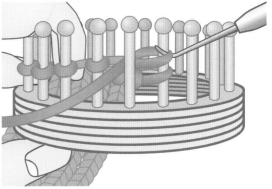

2 Move the loop from the second peg over to the first peg.

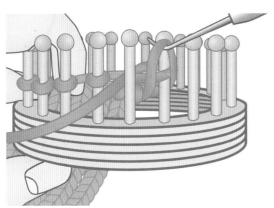

3 Knit over (lift bottommost loop up and off the peg).

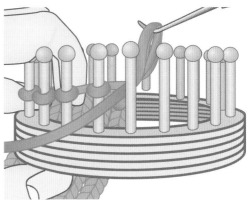

4 Move the loop on the first peg over to the peg just emptied. Knit the next peg.

Repeat steps 2–4 until you have cast off the required number of stitches. A stitch will remain on the last peg. Cut the working yarn leaving a 12.5cm (5in) tail. E-wrap the peg and knit over – pull the tail end through the stitch.

Yarn Over Cast Off

The Yarn Over Cast Off provides a stretchy border, perfect for items that require a flexible opening like magic scarves, ruffles, leggings, or the neckline of children's sweaters.

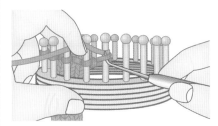

1 Knit the first stitch (peg 1).

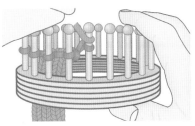

2 Wrap the peg in a clockwise direction.

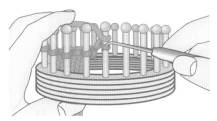

3 Knit over and knit the next stitch (peg 2).

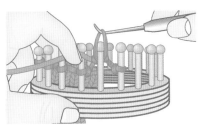

4 Move loop from peg 2 to peg 1. Knit over. Move loop from peg 1 to peg 2. Repeat steps 2–4. When one stitch remains, cut yarn leaving a tail. E-wrap the peg, knit over, and pull the tail end through.

Weaving in the Tail Ends

You have finished your first project, it is almost ready to be worn, but you still need to hide those unsightly tail ends of yarn. What to do?

It is fairly simple – all you need is a large tapestry needle. Work carefully on the wrong side of the item and your stitches should be invisible.

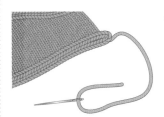

1 Locate the yarn tail end and thread it through the large eye of a tapestry needle.

2 Working on the wrong side of the item weave the yarn tail end by inserting the needle through the 'bump' of each knit stitch. Go up and down one row for about 3cm (1¹/₈in) in each direction.

Steps 1–2 should create a 'Z' with the tail end. Cut the remaining yarn as close to the knitted item as possible. Repeat this process with each yarn tail end you have in your knitted item.

Brim It

Brims/cuffs are not only for hats: get creative and place a small cuff at the top of your slippers, socks, or you can even make a small cuff on the beginning edge of a sweater. Creating a cuff or brim on your knitted hats can make them even warmer during the chilliest months. All you need do is knit for a few inches, then place the cast-on edge back on the knitting loom. Calculate how broad you would like your cuff to be, usually about 5–7.5cm (2–3in) (see the chart below).

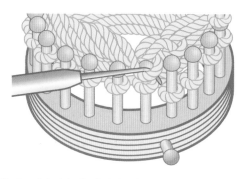

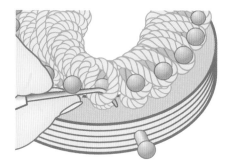

1 Reach inside the knitting loom, and find the beginning yarn tail end. Align the beginning yarn tail end with the first peg on the knitting loom. Next to the beginning tail end, locate the very first cast on stitch. Place the stitch on the corresponding peg. Repeat this step with the remaining stitches. Each peg should have two loops on it.

2 Knit over by lifting the bottom loop off the peg. After all the stitches have been knitted over, the loom should only have one loop on each peg. Continue knitting the hat in your pattern stitch.

Popular Cuff/Brim Lengths				
Cuff Length	7.5cm (3in)	6.5cm (2.5in)	5cm (2in)	2.5cm (1in)
Knit	15cm (6in)	12.5cm (5in)	10cm (4in)	5cm (2in)

TIP

You can hide the yarn tail end by sandwiching it between the layers of the cuff. When you bring up the cast-on edge for a cuff, simply place it inside the fold.

Making I-Cords on a Loom

Cords can be made on spools, or any circular knitting loom that is small enough to be worked like a small spool knitter, or you can create I-cords by using a round loom as a rake.

3-Stitch I-cord

Note that I-cord is knitted with the Knit Stitch. Work the loom in a clockwise direction (right to left).

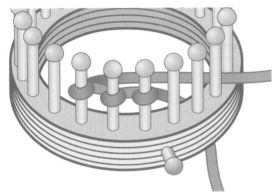

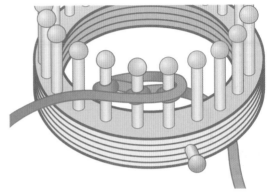

1 Cast on 3 pegs. With working yarn coming from the third peg run the yarn behind the pegs to the first peg.

2 Bring the yarn to the front of the loom ready to knit the 3 pegs.

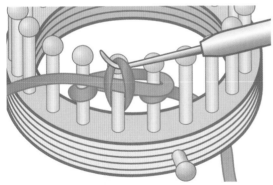

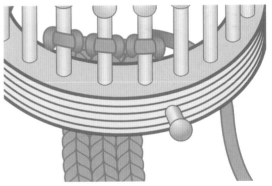

3 Knit the second peg, then the first, and the third one last. Repeat steps 1–3 until the cord measures the desired length.

4 Cast off by cutting the yarn, leaving a 10cm (4in) tail. Move the loop from peg 2 to peg 1. Knit over. Move the loop on peg 1 to peg 2. Move the loop on peg 3 to peg 2. Knit over. With working yarn, e-wrap peg 2. Knit over. Pull the last loop off the peg and pull on the yarn tail end.

TIP

Pull on the cord every couple of rows to set the stitches.

Let's Talk Tension

Let's take a small break and look at some numbers. Don't be scared and run away, but do feel free to reach for a little chocolate to calm your nerves. It's not algebra, honest.

When following a pattern, matching the tension is imperative, unless fit is not a factor. For this reason alone, it is recommended that you **always knit a swatch** before embarking on any project – especially if it needs to fit a certain someone.

Let's Make a Swatch

To loom knit a swatch, cast on the number of stitches called for in the tension section of the pattern plus 10 more. If the tension for the pattern states 4 stitches over 2 inches, then cast on 14 stitches. Loom knit the swatch using the stitch called for in the pattern until it reaches about 15cm (6in) in length, then cast off.

Measure for tension, counting all stitches; remember quarter stitches and half stitches count! Measure in two or three different places to make sure that the tension is consistent.

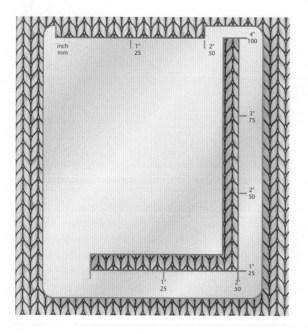

Got Tension
You can go forth and start loom knitting. Count yourself lucky!

More stitches per cm/inch than called for in the pattern. What does this mean? It means that if you go forth and knit with this yarn and knitting loom the item may be too small.
Fixer-uppers:
• Try with a thicker yarn.
• Try with a larger tension knitting loom.

Fewer stitches per inch/cm than called for in the pattern. What does this mean? It means that if you are stoic enough to continue, you will end up with an item that may be big enough to fit Goliath!
Fixer-uppers:
• Try with a thinner yarn.
• Try a smaller tension knitting loom.

Remember that stitch tension guide we talked about in the tools section? Well, it is time to take it out for a spin (see page 14). If you don't have one, you could also use a measuring tape.

Knit a small swatch to try out the stitches. Set it on a flat surface. Set the stitch guide in the centre of the swatch, placing it so there is a row aligned to the horizontal part of the L-shaped window.

Count the number of stitches along the horizontal side of the L-shaped window. Write the number down. Now, count the rows along the vertical side of the L-shaped window. Write down the number. The numbers that you come up with are your tension for that loom, using the type of yarn in the project, and the stitch used in the project. In the diagram on page 40, for example, there are 10 stitches per 5cm (2in) across and 19 rows per 10cm (4in) down.

Tension is dependent upon 4 factors:
• Yarn
• Tension of the knitting loom
• Type of stitch
• Your personal wrapping tension

The three first elements will have the most impact upon tension. If any of these three elements change, the tension will change.

Playing with Numbers

If your heart is set on a specific yarn but you still don't get tension, don't despair, you can continue forth. Bring out the calculator and do some maths and calculate the number of stitches and rows you will need in order to create the same item.

Let's assume you want to knit a square that is 51 x 51cm (20 x 20in). The tension given in the pattern is 6 stitches and 8 rows in 5 x 5cm (2 x 2in).

To create the square with the tension above you will need to cast on 60 stitches and knit for 80 rows. But, your swatch tells you that you've got a tension of 4 stitches and 6 rows in a 5 centimetre/2 inch square.

To create the square of 51 x 51cm (20 x 20in) you will need to make the following changes: cast on 40 pegs and knit 60 rows.

I know it is a bit frustrating knitting swatches but it is worth taking the time to knit a small swatch. Don't look at your swatches as lost time or yarn since you can always make something with them. Make small bags by knitting a rectangular swatch, then fold the rectangle in half. Seam the sides of the rectangle with a Mattress Stitch seam (see page 51). Knit a long cord (see I-Cord, page 39) and attach it to the bag and ta-da! Your swatch became a little bag.

Below: Each stitch affects the tension differently. For instance, the Single Stitch here has slightly lopsided Vs and will create a different tension to one formed by any other stitch you might choose.

More Cast Ons

In this section, we will look into more ways of casting on (CO). Each cast on method has recommended applications. The Cable and Chain cast on methods are the most useful.

Cable Cast On

This creates a neat, non-loopy, thick, cable-like flexible edge. The Cable Cast On sets your first row and it contains your very first knitted row.

It is recommended for items where the first row needs to be firm and it will be in prominent view as in the cast on for hats.

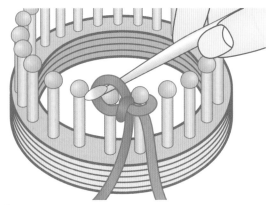

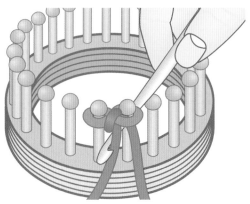

1 Make a slip knot; place it on the first peg. Take the working yarn to the outside of the loom. Using a crochet hook, insert the tip through the slip knot on the starting peg, hooking the working yarn and forming a loop. Place the loop made on the adjacent peg to the left.

2 With the crochet hook, go below the travelling yarn (between the first peg and second peg wrapped), hook the working yarn and pull towards the inside of the loom and towards the third peg. Place the loop from the hook on the next adjacent empty peg (peg 3).

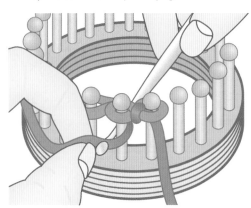

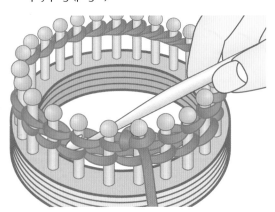

3 Repeat step 2 all around the loom. When you reach the last peg, place that last loop formed on the first peg.

4 Note how the front of each peg has two loops, while the inside only shows one. E-wrap the first peg with the working yarn. Knit over the two lowest strands off the peg, leaving only one loop on the peg. Knit over the bottommost loop on all the remaining pegs.

Chain Cast On

It provides a neat, flexible, non-loopy, crochet-like edge. It is similar to the Cable Cast On, except for its flexibility. It is a good overall cast on.

It is also used when an item calls for cast on stitches at the beginning or end of the next row on flat panels.

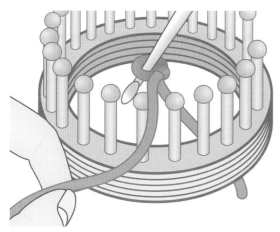

1 Form a slip knot with your yarn. Insert crochet hook through slip knot with the hook towards the centre of the knitting loom and the working yarn on the outside of the loom.

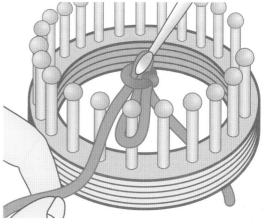

2 Place hook between the first two pegs. Hook the working yarn and pull the working yarn through the slip knot that is on the crochet hook (thus, wrapping the post of the peg).

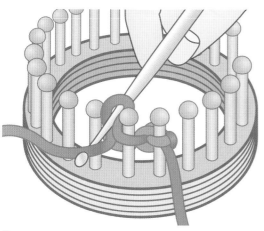

3 With crochet hook towards the inside of the loom, move up between the next set of pegs (between the second and third peg) and repeat step 2, continuing all around the loom.

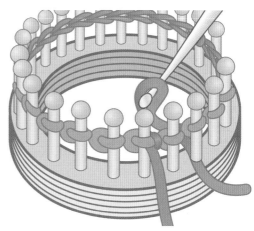

4 When you reach the last peg, take the loop on the hook and place it on the first peg. The knitting loom is ready to be knitted on.

Knit and Purl

The two basic stitches are the Knit, or Plain, and Purl Stitches. With these two techniques under your belt you will be able to create numerous stitch pattern for your loom knits.

Knit Stitch (k)

The Knit Stitch is the cornerstone of any loom-knitted item. Known also as the Flat or Plain Stitch, the Knit Stitch resembles the Knit Stitch created on knitting needles. It looks like a small V. In preparation the knitting loom must have at least one stitch on each peg (a cast on row).

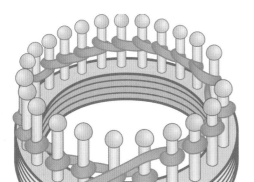

1 Lay the working yarn in front and above the stitch on the peg.

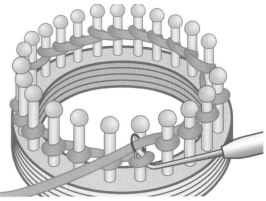

2 Insert the knitting tool through the stitch on the peg from bottom up. You are going to hook the working yarn where indicated by the red arrow.

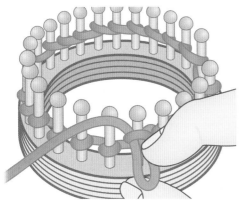

3 Hook the working yarn with knitting tool, making a loop. Grab the loop with your fingers.

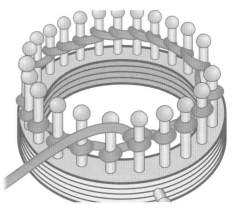

4 Take the original loop off the peg and replace with the new. Gently tighten the working yarn. Repeat steps 1–4 on each peg in turn to complete a knit row.

Purl Stitch (p)

The Purl Stitch is the reverse of a Knit Stitch and shows as a small horizontal bump on the front.

In preparation the knitting loom must have at least one stitch on each peg (a cast on row).

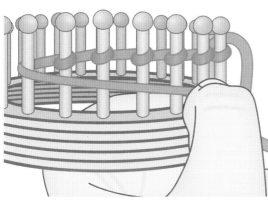

1 Lay the working yarn in front of and below the stitch on the peg.

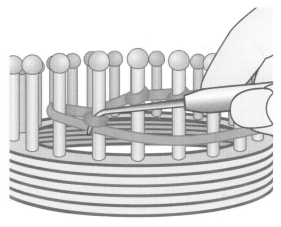

2 Insert the knitting tool from top to bottom through the stitch on the peg and scoop up the working yarn with the knitting tool.

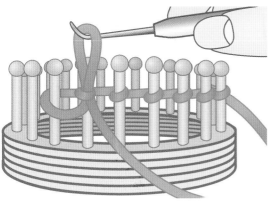

3 Pull the working yarn through the stitch on the peg to form a loop. Hold the new loop with your fingers.

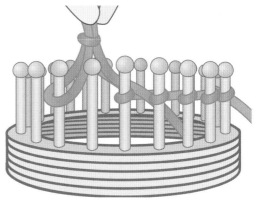

4 Take the old loop off the peg and place the new loop on the peg. Tug gently on the working yarn to tighten the stitch. Repeat 1–4 on each peg in turn to complete a purl row.

Basic Knit and Purl Combinations

Here is a small selection of basic Knit and Purl combinations. The patterns are written for flat panel and circular knitting, as well as in chart form. See pages 146–51 for more stitches.

Stocking Stitch (St st)
Multiple of 1 stitch

The Stocking Stitch pattern provides a flat fabric with a smooth right side and a bumpy wrong side.

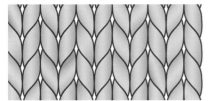

When knitting in Stocking Stitch your knitting will curl at the edges. It is the nature of the stitch to curl. To prevent curling, knit a Rib or Garter stitch edging.

How to: Knit every row/round				
4	K	K	K	K	
	K	K	K	K	3
2	K	K	K	K	
	K	K	K	K	1

Reverse Stocking Stitch (rev St st)
Multiple of 1 stitch

The reverse Stocking Stitch provides a textured fabric with a bumpy right side and a smooth wrong side.

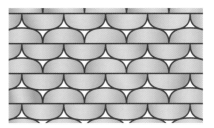

Circular and Flat Knitting:
St st: Knit every round/row
rev St st: Purl every round/row.

4	P	P	P	P	
	P	P	P	P	3
2	P	P	P	P	
	P	P	P	P	1

Garter Stitch (g st)
Multiple of 1 stitch

Garter stitch produces a reversible fabric – both sides will look the same. The two rows together will show on your knitted project as a row of horizontal bumps. Count each row of horizontal bumps as 2 knitted rows but 1 row of Garter Stitch.

4	P	P	P	P	
	K	K	K	K	3
2	P	P	P	P	
	K	K	K	K	1

Circular knitting:
Round 1: Purl the entire round.
Round 2: Knit the entire round.
Repeat rounds 1–2.

Flat Knitting:
Row 1: Knit to end.
Row 2: Purl to end.
Repeat Rows 1–2.

Rib Stitch (rib)

Rib Stitch produces a reversible fabric with vertical columns of stitches. It is a stretchable stitch, recommended for use whenever a snug fit is required, as in cuffs, sweater hems, necklines.

There are many variations of the Rib Stitch; presented below are some of the most commonly used.

1 x 1 Rib Stitch. Multiple of 2 stitches. Knitting Loom must have an even number of pegs.

Circular Knitting:

Rnd 1: *K1, p1. Repeat from * to end of row/rnd.

Consequent rows: Repeat row 1.

(knit the Knits, purl the Purls)

Flat Panel Knitting:

Row 1: *K1, p1; repeat from * to end.

Row 2: *P1, k1; repeat from * to end.

4	P	K	P	K	
	P	K	P	K	3
2	P	K	P	K	
	P	K	P	K	1

2 x 2 rib stitch. Multiple of 4 stitches + 2

4	P	P	K	K	
	P	P	K	K	3
2	P	P	K	K	
	P	P	K	K	1

Moss Stitch

Multiple of 2 stitches worked over 2 rows. Also known as Seed Stitch, Moss Stitch provides you with a textured, reversible fabric.

Circular Knitting:

Rnd 1: *K1, p1, rep from * to the end.

Rnd 2: *P1, k1, rep from * to the end.

Flat Knitting:

Row 1–2: *K1, p1, rep from * to the end.

Repeat these 2 rows.

2	K	P	K	P	
	P	K	P	K	1

Double Moss Stitch

Multiple of 2 stitches worked over 4 rows. Double Moss Stitch is a richly textured stitch, often seen on baby blankets or in combination with cables. It produces a reversible fabric.

Circular Knitting:

Rnds 1 and 2: *K1, p1, repeat from * to the end of the round.

Rnds 3 and 4: *P1, k1, repeat from * to the end of the round.

Repeat these 4 rows.

Flat Knitting:

Row 1 and 4: *K1, p1, repeat from * to the end.

Row 2 and 3: *P1, k1, repeat from * to the end.

4	K	P	K	P	
	K	P	K	P	3
2	P	K	P	K	
	P	K	P	K	1

Casting off

Although it is the last step in creating the knitted item, casting off holds as much importance as any other part of the piece and has impact on how the final item will look.

Single Crochet Cast Off

The Single Crochet Cast Off gathers the stitches together for a tapered edge. Recommended on sleeves that require a firm edge.

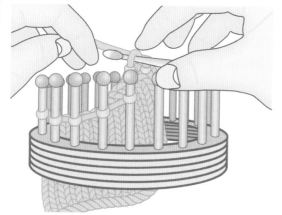

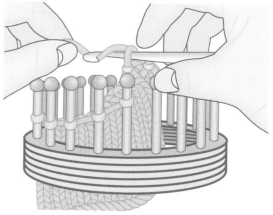

1 Use a crochet hook, the size recommended for your yarn. Start at the side where the working yarn is located. With the working yarn on the left, and crochet hook on the right, remove the stitch from the peg with the crochet hook.

2 Hook the working yarn with the crochet hook; pull the yarn through the stitch to make a loop.

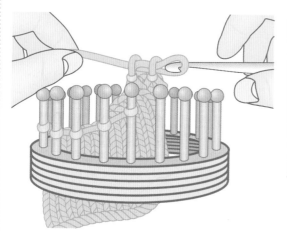

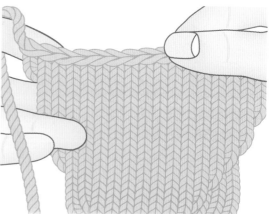

3 Repeat 1–2 into the next stitches, making sure to pass the new loop formed through both the stitch being cast off and the stitch on the hook.

4 When you reach the last stitch, cut the working yarn, leaving a 12.5cm (5in) tail. Hook the tail through the last stitch to lock it in place.

Double Crochet Cast Off

Here you crochet one chain between each loop removed from the knitting loom. It provides a firm, non-tapered edge, recommended for items that require a flexible finish. Using the hook size recommended for your yarn, start at the side where the working yarn is located.

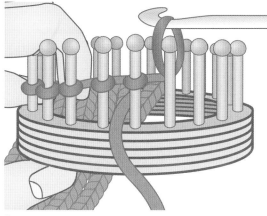

1 With the loom in your left hand, and crochet hook in your right, remove the stitch from the peg with the crochet hook.

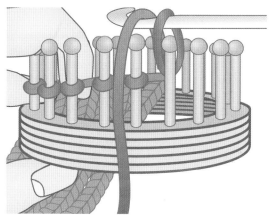

2 Hook the working yarn with the crochet hook; pull the yarn through the stitch on the hook to make a loop.

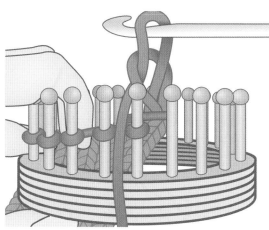

3 Make 1 chain (crochet 1 chain by wrapping the yarn around the hook and bringing it through the loop on the hook).

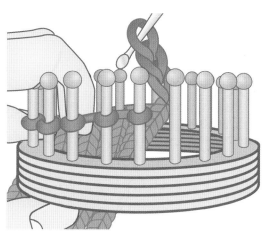

4 Move to the next peg to the right and repeat steps 1–3. When you reach the last stitch, cut the working yarn leaving a 12.5cm (5in) tail, hook the tail and pass it through the last stitch to lock it in place.

Linking Cast Offs

Sometimes you will need to join two panels together while casting off. Below are two methods, one involves using knitting needles and the other is done on a knitting loom.

Three-Needle Cast Off

You will need 3 knitting needles or 2 knitting needles and 1 crochet hook. Transfer the stitches from the knitting loom onto one of the knitting needles. Transfer the stitches from the other panel to the second knitting needle. Hold the two needles together, right sides together. The two knitting needles should be held in one hand together, both pointing in the same direction.

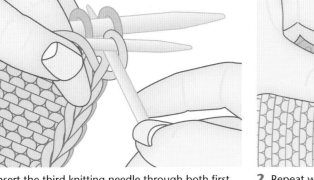

1 Insert the third knitting needle through both first stitches and knit them together.

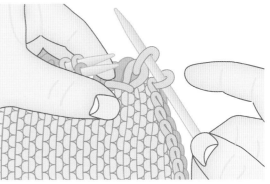

2 Repeat with the next set of two stitches.

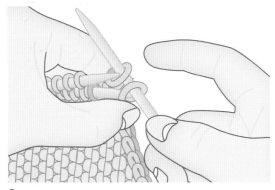

3 Pass the first stitch on the right (third) knitting needle over the second stitch – 1 stitch cast off.

With Crochet Hook

1 Insert the crochet hook through both first stitches (front needle and back needle), hook the working yarn and pull through the two stitches.
2 Repeat with the next set of two stitches.
3 Pass the front stitch through the back stitch – 1 stitch cast off.

Both Methods

Repeat steps 1–3 until all stitches have been cast off. Cut the working yarn and pull through the last stitch.

Grafting

Another useful linking method, sometimes known as Kitchener Stitch, grafting is often used on the toe of socks as it doesn't create an uncomfortable ridge. You will need two knitting needles, set up as step 1 above. Cut the working yarn keeping a long tail, and thread the end through a tapestry needle.

1 Take the yarn through the first stitch on the needle closest to you as if to purl, then through the first stitch on the second needle, as if you were going to knit it.
2 Slip these two stitches off their needles. Gently pull the yarn to tighten the stitch, but don't pull too much.
3 Repeat steps 1–2 until you reach the end of the rows.
4 Weave in the ends to the wrong side.

Joining Two Panels on a Knitting Loom

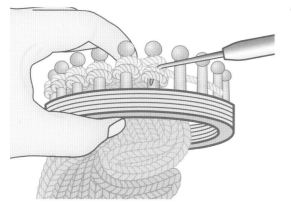

1 Remove panels from the knitting loom and place the stitches on a stitch holder. Place one of the panels back on the knitting loom with the right side facing the inside of the loom; the wrong side will be facing you. Pay close attention to putting the stitches back on the knitting loom correctly. Place the second panel on the knitting loom by placing the stitches on the same pegs that the first panel is occupying, right sides of the panels together.

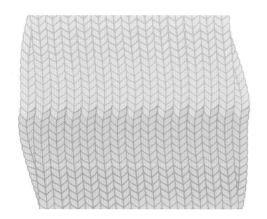

2 Follow the Basic Cast Off method on page 36 and cast off the stitches – knit through both stitches on the pegs (lay working yarn above the two stitches on the peg, insert knitting tool through the two stitches, catch the working yarn and pull through the two stitches, hold the loop formed by the working yarn, take the two stitches off the peg and place the newly formed loop on the peg).

Mattress Stitch

Once you are loom knitting flat panels you will need to join your seams. Mattress Stitch is a neat stitch, which can hardly be seen from the right side. It is advisable to use the same yarn that you knitted with, unless you want the stitches to be a feature of your work.

1 Lay the pieces to be joined right side up and side by side. Thread a tapestry needle with the tail end. Bring the yarn through to the front, in the middle of the first stitch on the first row of the seam. Take the needle through to the same position on the other piece, and bring it out in the middle of the edge stitch one row up.

2 Insert the needle back into the first piece of fabric, in the same place that the yarn last came out. Then bring the needle out in the middle of the stitch above. Repeat this, making a zigzag seam from edge to edge for a few more rows. You can pull the thread firmly, and the stitches almost disappear. When the seam is finished, weave in the ends.

Dropped it... Fixing Mistakes

So you have been happily knitting, then you look down and – horror – you see a stitch dangling all by itself. What do you do? If it is one or two stitches, we can save the day.

Picking Up a Dropped Stitch

As soon as you spot the dropped stitch, hold it in place with a safety pin or stitch holder; failure to do so will cause the stitch to drop further down the column. Knit to the peg next to the dropped stitch. Now the scary part: unravel the stitch on the same column where the dropped stitch is located; it will stop unravelling when you reach the dropped stitch. Then get a crochet hook...

On Stocking Side Fabric

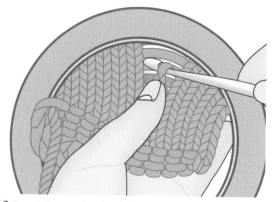

1 Insert the crochet hook from front to back through the dropped stitch.

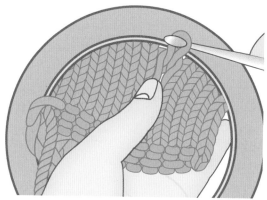

2 Hook the first 'ladder' or horizontal bar behind the stitch and pull it through the stitch to the front of the work.

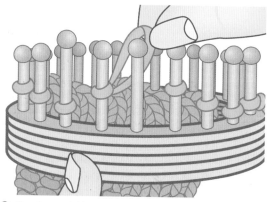

3 Continue picking up the unraveled stitches by following step 2. When all stitches have been picked up, place the last stitch back on the peg.

On Purl Side Fabric

1 Insert the crochet hook through the back of the fabric (inside the circle of the loom, or the wrong side of the fabric). Hook the dropped stitch.

2 Hook the unravelled strand behind the stitch and pull it through the stitch to the back of the fabric.

3 Continue picking up the unravelled stitches by following step 2. When all stitches have been picked up, place the last stitch back on the peg.

Fixing Stitches

If you accidentally knitted the wrong stitch on the row below, you have two options:

Option 1: Tink back the row, one stitch at a time, until you reach the stitch where the mistake is located. Fix the stitch and continue knitting.

Option 2: Drop the stitch on that column of stitches and unravel to fix the mistake.

GLOSSARY

Tink is the process of undoing a row by undoing a stitch at a time – it is the word knit spelled backwards.

If the problem is located a few rows back, it is best to unravel the knitting and undo the entire row with the mistake.

1 Use a piece of waste yarn or a circular needle to hold your stitches to act as a lifeline one row below the problem row.

2 Take the stitches off the pegs and unravel all the stitches until you reach the row with the lifeline that is your stitch holder.

3 Place the stitches back on the pegs. Make sure to position the stitches on the loom the correct way. Twist them if you were knitting the Twisted Knit Stitch. Don't twist them if you were knitting the Knit Stitch.

Joining Yarns

When you least expect it, it happens – the yarn suddenly comes to an end, or worse, breaks. It is time to attach a new yarn to the project.

At the Edge: Join the new yarn at the beginning of a row. If possible join the yarn on an edge that will be within a seam.

Method 1: Leave at tail of about 12.5–15cm (5–6in) in length on the old skein and another tail the same length on the new skein. Hold the two yarns together and knit the first three stitches. Drop the old skein and continue knitting with the newly joined yarn.

Method 2: Leave a tail of about 12.5–15cm (5–6in) in length on the old skein and another tail the same length on the new skein. Tie a temporary knot with the two ends as close to the project as possible. Pick up the newly joined yarn and continue knitting. When the project is complete, go back and undo the knot, weave in the ends in the opposite direction to close the gap formed by the change of yarns.

Stuck in the Middle: Occasionally you will need to join yarn in the middle of a row. In this case, you can use Method 2. Tie a temporary knot close to the garment; make sure to leave a 12.5–15cm (5–6in) tail on both ends. Continue knitting from the new yarn. Make sure to undo the knot before weaving in the ends.

 TIP

If you encounter a knot in your yarn, do not knit with it. Cut it and join the yarn using one of the methods above.

Creating Flat Panels

Don't feel intimidated by the idea of creating a flat panel on a circular loom. It is a simple process that involves knitting on the knitting loom in a 'C' figure.

From A to B and Back Again...

Knitting a flat panel on the knitting loom is not much different from knitting circularly on the knitting loom. You can do the same cast on methods, knit the same stitches, and use the same cast off methods.

However, there are a few things that differ. Since you are not knitting circularly around the knitting loom, you will have a starting point and an ending point. At both ends you will have a turning peg/stitch marking the beginning of a new row or the end of the last one.

When starting at point A, the peg at point A is your beginning peg. The peg at point B becomes your last peg, and will also be your turning peg. When you finish a row, by knitting the peg at point B, you turn and knit back to point A. Thus the pegs and Point A and B alternate as turning pegs and beginning and ending pegs for the rows.

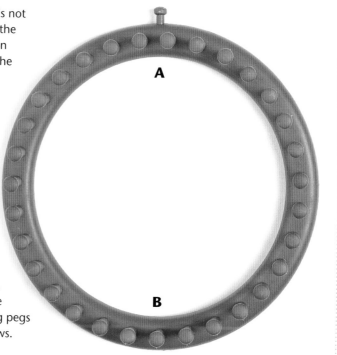

Beware of the Selvedge

Now you are no longer going round in circles, you will have edges to deal with. The edge stitches of a knitted panel are called Edge or Selvedge Stitches.

When knitting from a pattern, look for instructions on how to treat the Selvedge Stitches. One way is to wrap the turning pegs and knit them. Alternatively you can Slip Stitch the first stitch on each row.

A Slip Stitch (sl st) is simply a stitch that is not knitted. You skip the peg and simply take the yarn to the next peg and knit it. Using a Slip Stitch at the beginning of each row creates a chain-like edge at both sides of the knitted item.

How to decide which turning option to use? If you are going to be seaming two pieces together or adding a border, it is best to knit the edge stitches (always knit the first and last stitches).

If you are looking for a more decorative edging, slip the first stitch of every row. However, slipping the stitch on each row will narrow the width of your knitted item by two stitches. If the pattern doesn't allow for this, you will have to add one stitch to either side of the pattern.

GLOSSARY

Selvedge As its name suggests, this is the self-made edge of the fabric you are creating, sometimes disappearing in a seam, but sometimes a more visible finished edge.

Turning Stitch Options

You can knit the first peg, or slip it. Knitting the knit stitch or the twisted knit stitch at the beginning and end of each row provides a nice even edge.

To begin a practice piece, cast a few stitches on your knitting loom in a clockwise direction.

Using the Twisted Knit Stitch

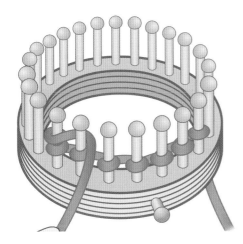

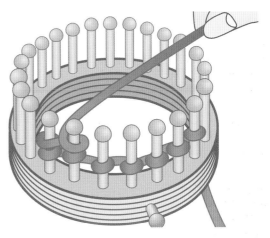

1 E-wrap the last peg in an anticlockwise direction, run the working yarn behind to the next peg and wrap around it in a clockwise direction. KO this stitch, then go back and knit over the turning peg. Tug the yarn gently to tighten the first stitch.

2 Continue working down the row, E-Wrapping the pegs in a clockwise direction, then knit over the bottom loop up and off the peg.

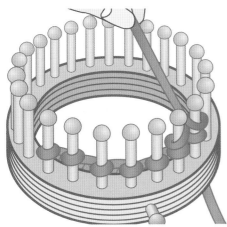

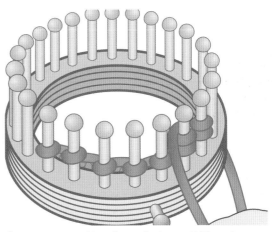

3 Next row: bring the working yarn clockwise to the front of the first peg. E-wrap the next peg, to the left, in an anticlockwise direction. Go back to the first peg and knit over. Tug gently on the working yarn to tighten the first stitch.

4 Continue working down the loom, E-Wrapping the pegs in an anticlockwise direction.

Shaping

With the aid of essential increases and decreases, we can create knitted fabric that fits comfortably. Shaping can remove or add stitches to allow a more fitted fabric.

Increases (inc)

Adding extra stitches to the panel makes it wider. When increases happen within rows, it is recommended to only increase 2 stitches on a given row. Increases are used to shape items such as sweater sleeves, skirts, and any items that fan out. There are various ways to increase stitches on the loom, and all of them require you to move the stitches outwards to the empty pegs to allow room, or an empty peg, for the new stitch. Here you will find three methods. Familiarise yourself with all three.

Make 1 (M1)

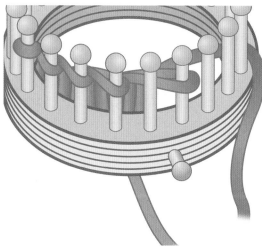
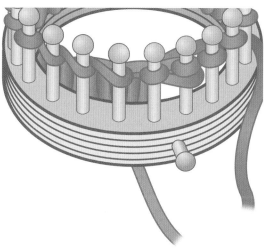

1 Move the last stitch to the next empty peg outwards, leaving an empty peg between the last peg and the peg before last.

2 Make 1 (M1): Work the stitches on the knitting loom, and when you reach the empty peg, look behind it and reach for the horizontal bar coming from the pegs either side of the empty peg. Hook this horizontal bar with the knit hook and place it to the front of the peg. Knit the peg (with the stitch specified in the pattern: either e-wrap, knit stitch, or purl stitch). Continue knitting to the end of the row.

Creating an increase in this manner will leave a small hole. To avoid the hole, twist the horizontal bar, forming a small loop, and place this loop on the peg.

> **TIP**
> When creating a piece that will require many increases, make sure to cast on to a loom that is big enough to hold all the stitches you'll need.

Smart Shaping

As a new loom knitter, the tendency will be to simply cast on the desired number of additional stitches at the end of the row rather than increase within the row. By increasing within the row, the knitted item maintains its edge shaping.

The increasing techniques here are recommended whenever you need to increase one or two stitches within a row. Casting on is recommended when increasing more than two stitches on the edge of the row. You couldn't make a shape like this fish without increasing and decreasing.

Lifted Increase Make 1

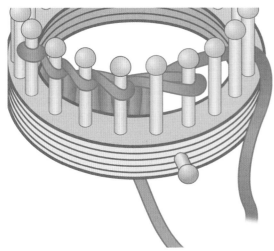

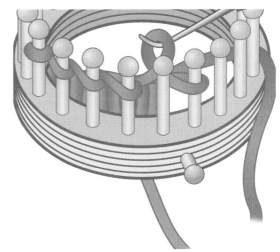

1 Move the last stitch outwards to the next empty peg, leaving an empty peg between the last peg and the peg before last.

2 With the knitting tool, reach for the running-ladder coming from the two stitches on either side below the empty peg. Twist the strand and place it on the empty peg (if you don't twist it, you will create a small hole). Knit your row as usual.

Row Below

This is another way of increasing using a crochet hook.

1 Move the last stitch to the next empty peg outwards, leaving an empty peg between the last peg and the peg before last. Get a crochet hook.

2 Knit to the empty peg, and with the crochet hook reach one stitch below (on the wrong side), pass the hook through one of the 'legs' of the stitch and hook the working yarn making a loop. Place the loop on the empty peg. Make sure to not pull on the stitch below too much as this may cause the stitch to pull together. Knit the row as usual.

Decreases (dec)

Removing stitches from your panel will make the panel narrower. When decreases happen within rows it is recommended to decrease 1 or 2 stitches in from either edge to keep the selvedge neat. There are various ways to decrease on the knitting loom; all of them require you to move the stitches inwards. Familiarise yourself with the methods below.

Knit 2 Together (k2tog)

Knitting 2 together (k2tog) creates a right-slanting decrease, and is best created at the beginning of a knit row.

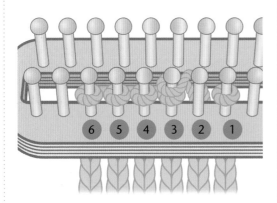

Move the stitch from peg 2 to peg 3 (the peg to its left). Peg 3 now has two stitches and peg 2 is empty.
Note: the stitch from peg 3 will be on the bottom and the stitch from peg 2 is on top. When knitting over, the stitch that was on peg 2 will disappear behind the stitch from peg 3.
Move stitches inwards so there are no empty pegs. Knit the row as usual, making sure to knit 2 over 1 on the peg with the extra stitch.

Slip, Slip, Knit (ssk)

The left-slanting decrease is the mirror image of a k2tog and is achieved by a slip, slip, knit (ssk) at the end of a row.

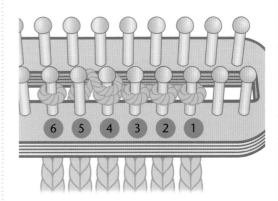

Move the stitch from peg 5 over to peg 4 (or the peg to its right).
Note: The stitch from the right peg (peg 4) is on the bottom, the stitch from the left peg (peg 5) is on top – do not change the order of the loops – keep the bottom loop on the bottom and the top on the top. Move stitches inwards so there are no empty pegs. Continue knitting as usual down the row.

Purl 2 Together (p2tog)

Also known as p2tog, this too creates a right-slanting decrease, best created at the beginning of a purl side row. It is made just like the k2tog above, except in a purl row. Purl the row as usual. When you reach the peg with the extra stitch, lay the yarn below the two loops, and purl them, making sure to remove the two loops off the peg and leaving the newly formed loop.

TIP

It is best to do all increases/decreases at least one or two stitches away from the edge. Creating the increases/decreases right on the edge can cause sloppy edges and it makes picking up stitches very difficult.

Increasing Two Stitches or More

In certain cases, a pattern will call for increasing more than two stitches at any given row. In this case, it is best to cast on the stitches using a method like the Chain Cast On method (see page 43).

Increasing more than two stitches at the beginning of the row:

1 Knit the entire row as called for in the pattern. With the working yarn coming from the last stitch, cast on to the empty pegs using the chain cast on method. When you reach the desired peg number, stop.

2 The loom is threaded with the extra stitches and is now ready. Turn back and knit or purl these stitches as directed by the pattern.

Decreasing Two Stitches or More

A pattern sometimes will ask you to cast off stitches at a certain point within the pattern.

Knit to the stitch where the casting off is supposed to begin. Start casting off using the Basic Cast Off method (see page 36), stop when you have bound off the number of stitches called for in the pattern.

Most patterns will let you know which increase or decrease method you should use. If there is no information about which method to use, knit a small swatch and experiment with the different methods above and see which one looks best. The decreases on a sleeve, for example, usually come in pairs – k2tog at the beginning of the row and ssk at the end – look for these mirror images whenever you are knitting something that has increases or decreases at each end.

Short Row Shaping

This allows shaping a knitted panel without the decreasing stitches. It creates soft curves by knitting a row to a certain stitch in the row, then turning back and knitting in the other direction. It is a method commonly used in heels, blouse darts for the stomach or bust area, and in any other item where you want seamless curves. Shaping with short rows has one pitfall that you must be aware of. It is necessary to wrap the stitch after the turning point to avoid a hole between the turning stitch and the next stitch. The 'wrap' eliminates this almost completely.

How to Wrap and Turn (W&T)

When knitting each wrapped peg, lift both the wrap and the stitch together, 2 over 1, as this will eliminate the wrap and fill the hole made with the short rows.

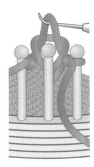

1 Knit or purl to the desired turning stitch. Take the stitch off the next peg and hold it with your knitting tool.

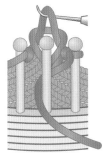

2 Wrap the peg by taking the yarn towards the inside of the loom and wrapping around the peg. The working yarn will end up to the front of the knitting loom.

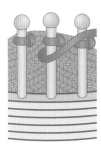

3 Place the stitch back on the peg. Take the working yarn and knit or purl back across the row.

Working with Colour

It is easy to jazz up a simple pattern by doing colour changes along the way. Take a chance and create a wild project with some odd skeins left from other projects.

Stripes

Creating stripes is the easiest method to spice up a project. Knitting with stripes allows you to use as many colours as you wish without having to carry more than one colour at a time within the row.

Designing with stripes is easy – gather all your odd skeins, choose ones of similar weight, sit down and loom knit a one-of-a-kind item. Keep the following suggestions in mind when creating your stripes:
• Wide stripes
• Narrow stripes
• Alternate between narrow and wide stripes
• Spice it up: mix wild colours and textured yarns

Stripy Goodness

Now that you have gathered all your odd skeins, it is time to sit down and knit your original item. Your one-of-a-kind creation will have one main colour (MC) with one (or more) contrasting colours (CC). When more than one contrasting colour is used, the colours are designated letters, such as A, B, C, D, and so on.

Knit a few rows with your main colour. When it's time to change to a new colour, join the new yarn at the beginning of a row (see Joining Yarns on page 53).

After you have your desired colours set up, you can carry the colour along the edge of the item if knitting thin stripes. If you are knitting wider stripes, cut the yarn at the end of a row, and join yarns at the beginning of a row.

When flat panel knitting, try to work the stripes in sets of two rows, then the yarn will end on the same side. If you work an uneven number of rows, you will find your yarn on the opposite side of your knitting and you will have to cut the yarn and join the yarn to the opposite edge.

Weaving In the Ends

Weave in the ends vertically along the edge of the item – through the same colour stripe as the yarn being woven. You can also weave in the ends to the wrong side of the item.

Going Up

Creating thin vertical stripes is simple, and weaving of yarns at the back of the work is not required. The unused yarn can be carried behind the work. To create thin vertical stripes, you will need yarn in two colours: a main colour (MC) and a contrasting colour (CC).

1 Pick up the main colour and knit the stitches you desire in the main colour, skip the ones you desire in contrasting colour.
2 Go back to the beginning of the row, pick up the contrasting colour and knit all the pegs skipped in step 1.
Repeat steps 1–2 throughout.

Weaving In the Ends

Weave in the ends horizontally along the edge of the item – through the same colour stripe as the yarn being woven.

Painting with Yarn

The art of Fair Isle loom knitting is a technique of multicoloured knitting, where a row is worked with only two colours in small repeating sections of colour patterns.

Traditional Fair Isle knitting is done completely in stocking stitch (knit every row in the round), two different colours per row, and the items are usually circular. The circular nature of the item helps to hide the floats created by the colour changes within the row. When carrying the unused colour, it is recommended to not carry it over more than 5–7 sts, or 2.5–4cm (1–1½in).

Fair Isle patterns are usually depicted in chart form and share some characteristics with regular knitting charts. Each square represents a stitch and will either be coloured in or will have a colour symbol and key.

For flat panel knitting, read the chart starting at the bottom, right side. Then move up to the second row, and read it from left to right. For circular knitting, read the chart starting at the bottom, right side. Continue reading the next rounds starting at the right side.

Loom Knitting Fair Isle

Although it may seem complicated, the process of painting with your yarn is quite simple. There are two methods that you can use. The first method keeps your yarns separated and untangled. You pick up the main colour at the beginning of a row, knit the required stitches then drop it at the end of the row. Pick up the contrasting colour and knit all the required stitches with that colour, then drop it. In the second method, you carry both yarns with

you in your dominant hand as you work the stitch pattern. When the pattern calls for the CC, drop the MC colour and bring the CC above the MC working yarn, knit as required. When the pattern calls for the MC, drop the CC, reach below for the MC colour. Every time you change yarns, drop the new one above then reach below for the other.

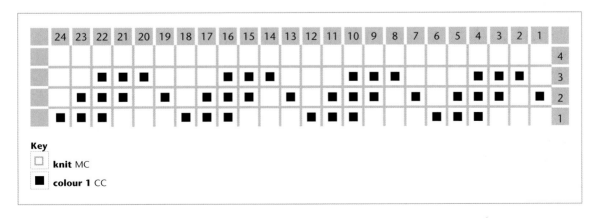

Key

☐ **knit** MC

■ **colour 1** CC

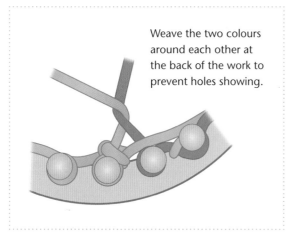

Weave the two colours around each other at the back of the work to prevent holes showing.

To minimize the length of the floats at the back of the work, it is advisable to weave the yarns around each other when travelling more than three stitches. To weave the yarns around each other: knit a few stitches with the MC, drop it and pick up the CC, wrap the CC around the MC, drop the CC, pick up the MC and keep on knitting. Take both colours to the back of the work, and twist them together (see diagram above).

Fair Isle allows you to create a wide range of complex colour designs. Sit down with some graph paper and different colouring pencils and try different colour combinations before trying it on the knitting loom. Have fun painting patterns with your yarn!

Fair Isle Characteristics
- 2 colours per row: main colour (MC) and the contrasting colour (CC)
- Stocking stitch
- Wrong side does not show

Mock Cables

Creating texture by twisting stitches is easier than it looks.

The principle of twisting stitches to create texture is fairly easy; it consists of two stitches interchanging places. No special tools are necessary. Every time stitches are crossed over one another, the knitted item shrinks horizontally, therefore twisting stitches makes the knitted piece narrower than knitting the same piece in stocking stitch.

Most of the time, you will encounter twisted stitch patterns knitted on stocking stitch on a background of reverse stocking. The background of purl stitches helps bring out the twisted stitches and give them a three-dimensional appearance.

The crossed stitches presented in this section are two-stitch twist patterns. They work well as part of a rib stitch pattern, or as borders to give a flat panel extra dimension.

There are two types of twists: right slanting and left slanting. They complement each other – if knitting a panel with a border at each side, you will place a right slanting cable on one side and the left slanting cable on the opposite side.

Let's get ready to do the twist – we will begin with the right-slanting twist (TW or RTW) on a reverse stocking background. We will assume that we are working on a knitting loom with 6 pegs, pegs will be numbered 1–6 (from right to left). Pegs 1 and 2 will be purled, pegs 3 and 4 will be

where the twist occurs, pegs 5 and 6 will be purled.

Classic Mock Cable instructions consist of the following 4 rows, and as you can see the twist only happens in one row, row 3, the other rows are knitted normally.
Row 1, 2, 4: p2, k2, p2.
Row 3: p2, TW, p2.

How to twist the stitches for right-slanting cable:
Take stitch from peg 3 off the knitting loom, hold it on your knitting tool, or on a cable needle, and place it towards the centre of the knitting loom. Move stitch from peg 4 to emptied peg 3. Place the stitch from the

cable needle on peg 4. Twist completed. After the twist is completed, knit the stitches as called for in the pattern.

How to twist the stitches for left-slanting cable:
Take stitch from peg 4 off the knitting loom, hold it on your knitting tool, or on a cable needle, and place it towards the centre of the knitting loom. Move stitch from peg 3 to emptied peg 4. Place the stitch from the cable needle on peg 3. Twist completed. After the twist is completed, knit the stitches as called for in the pattern.
Row 1, 2, 4: p2, k2, p2.
Row 3: p2, LTW, p2.

Sock Loom Knitting

Once you can knit and purl you can create beautiful knitted socks. Sock looms are compact enough to fit into a small bag and be carried along with you.

Sock Yarn

Yarn comes in different thicknesses from super chunky down to cobweb lace weight. The knitting loom tension will determine the thickness of yarn you can use for your socks. There are many yarns that are inexpensive and durable. Visit your local yarn store and browse through their sock yarn collection to get an idea of the different yarns available.

Did you know that yarn has memory? Items made with yarn that retains memory can return to their original shape after being stretched out. A yarn with good memory, like wool, is great for socks.

Sock Knitting Looms

Virtually any knitting loom that produces the size of tube needed can be used as a sock loom. However, to produce socks that you can wear with everyday shoes, you need a knitting loom with a very small gauge that provides a very tight knit tension. The socks completed for this book were done on two different tension looms: the Chunky Ribbed Socks (see page 100) and the Weekend Socks (see page 104) were completed on a 24 peg large gauge loom, the Mock Cable Socks (see page 102) were completed on 64 peg fine gauge loom. Whichever you choose – enjoy knitting your own socks.

To select the appropriate size knitting loom:

1 Place your foot on a flat surface.

2 Measure around the ball of the foot (the widest part below the toe line).

3 Write down the measurement.

Generally socks are knitted with a negative ease of 10–15%, so try to find a knitting loom that produces a tube 10–15% smaller than the measurement found above.

Cuff

The cuff is the first part of the sock that is knitted. It requires a flexible cast on to allow a good fit – the Cable Cast On (see page 42) is recommended.

The Anatomy of a Sock

Socks can be knitted either toe up, or top down. All the patterns in this book are for top down socks. The sock is knitted in one single piece; it starts in the round, then it is knitted flat for the heel, then it is knitted in the round again for the foot, and finally the toe is knitted flat, and grafted.

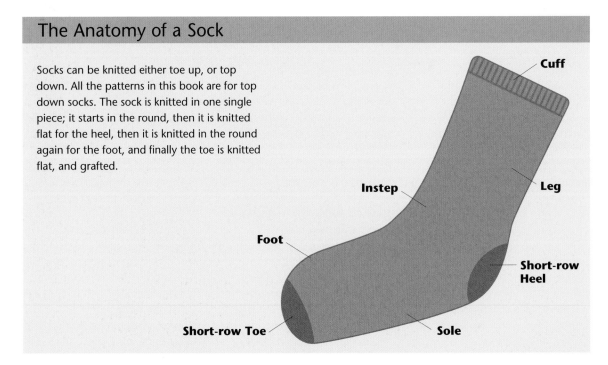

Cuff

Instep

Leg

Foot

Short-row Heel

Short-row Toe

Sole

Memory Yarn

Wool and nylon
Durable and strong with some memory.
Wool
Warm during winter, cool during summer.
Has memory which makes it less likely to
stretch out of shape.
Cotton
Cool during the summer. No memory.

Leg

The leg is knitted next and, like the cuff, needs to be
flexible, so a combination of ribbing and stocking
stitch is usually used.

Short-row Heel

The heel is where the magic takes place – this small
part is where the tube becomes a recognizable sock.
The heel is knitted as a flat panel with decreases and
increases to form an hourglass shape. The technique
of short-row shaping is used to create the decreases.

Foot

Once the heel is completed, the rest is fairly simple.
The foot is knitted in the round.

Toe

The toe is another magical part of our sock-making
technique. In this book's patterns, we will use the
same technique and the same numbers used in the
heel section to make the toe, what you will have is
a little cup that extends from the sole of the sock to
the top part of the sock. The one side of the cup will
need to be grafted to the top foot part of the sock.

The Short-row Technique

At first, when you begin knitting the heel, it looks like
just a small triangle, and then the triangle takes the
shape of a small cup. This element of magic is what
turns a simple tube into a cherished handknit sock.

The heel is created in two parts – a decreasing
part and an increasing part. The decreasing section
requires the knowledge of the Wrap and Turn
technique (W&T, see page 59). The increasing
section requires the knitter to knit over the wrap and
the stitch at the same time.

The term 'short row' means that a row is not
knitted to the end; instead, you will knit to a certain
point and stop. Then, you turn back and knit in
the other direction. However, if you knit to the
designated point, then turn back and knit in the
other direction, a small hole will be created at the
turning point. To avoid this hole, again we use
Wrap and Turn.

Designing Your Own Socks

Once you learn
the basics of sock
knitting, you will
probably want
to design your
own. Most of the
sock knitting is
straightforward; however, the heel needs
special attention. Keep the following general
guidelines in mind when designing your
own socks:
• Use half of the stitches on the knitting loom
  for the heel.
• Short-row down until one third of the pegs
  used for the heel are not W&T.
• For a narrower heel/wider heel – use fewer
  stitches/more stitches.
• The toe area is done exactly as the heel.
  At the end, close the toe by sewing.
Enjoy the magic of sock making!

Board Knitting

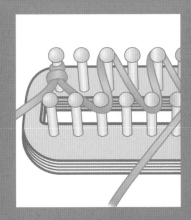

Knitting Boards

Get ready to create in double knit. Here you will learn the process of using a knitting board to create beautiful double-sided items that use both sides of the loom.

A knitting board is a frame that has two rows of pegs facing each other. The knitted garment passes through the centre of the frame and comes out the bottom of the frame. In order to create a double-sided item, you will weave yarn from one side of the board to the other side. A knitting board is also known as a double-sided rake. Consequently, a knitting board can also be used as a knitting rake – by using only one side.

Knitting Board Tensions and Yarns

The tension of the board is determined by the distance from centre of peg to centre of peg as well as by the distance between the two rows of pegs. The tension of the board will determine the type of yarn you can use on it. The desired look of the knitted garment will determine what type of board and yarn you would need to use.

Currently there is no standard knitting board tension terminology among loom manufacturers, and one vendor's regular tension may be equivalent to another vendor's large tension. The following are general guidelines on the yarn types to use on the different knitting boards available.

Large Tension
1 strand of bulky weight yarn or 2 strands of Aran weight yarn.
Regular Tension
1 strand of Aran weight yarn.
Small Tension
1 strand of DK weight yarn.
Fine Tension
1 strand of 2-ply or sock weight yarn.

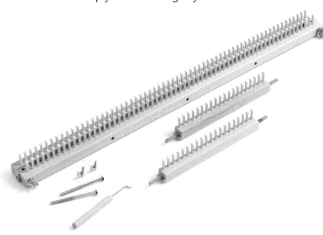

The Knitting Board

Some notes before we embark on our double knit adventure:
- A knitting board has two rows of pegs facing each other. For demonstration purposes, we will name one side, side A, the opposite side, side B.
- The pegs will be numbered as 1A, 1B, 2A, 2B; each pair of pegs is known as a set.
- Work on the board from left to right.

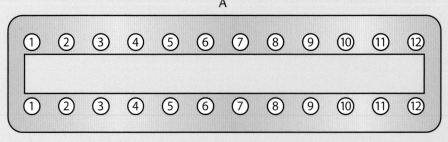

Basic Cast On

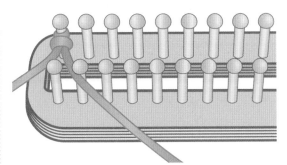

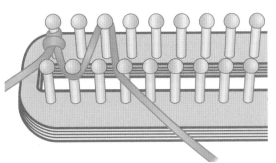

1 Make a slip knot and place it on the first top peg of the knitting board (peg 1A).

2 Take the working yarn down to peg 2B, wrap around it. Go up to peg 3A, wrap around it, then down to peg 4B, wrap around it. Continue in this manner, skipping every other peg, until you reach the end of the board (or the number of stitches you want to cover for your pattern).

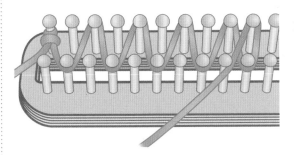

3 To complete the circular go to the peg directly across, wrap it. Continue wrapping the pegs that were skipped in step 1.

Anchor Yarn

Place a piece of contrasting yarn in the middle of the board. The yarn is called an anchor yarn and needs to be long enough to thread the ends down through the centre gap of the board and tie them together, thus securing the cast-on row of stitches.

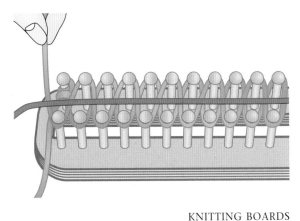

The anchor yarn has two purposes:
1 It aids in pulling your item down the centre of the board.
2 It helps you identify the live stitches that you will be casting off later.

Knitting Board Stitches

Once your cast on row is finished you are ready to begin knitting with the desired pattern stitch. Take your pick from the ones below.

Basic Stocking Stitch

Basic stocking is achieved by wrapping the board in the same manner as the cast on row on the previous page.

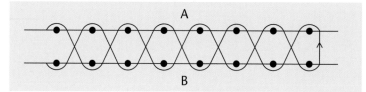

Start at peg 1A. Take the working yarn down to peg 2B, and wrap around it. Go up to peg 3A, wrap around it, then down to peg 4B, wrap around it, and continue in this manner, skipping every other peg, until you reach the end of the board (or the number of stitches you want to include for your pattern). To complete the circular, go to the peg directly across from the final peg, wrap it, and continue back along the loom, wrapping the pegs that were skipped in Step 1.

Knit Over Process: Start by knitting the first 2 sets of pegs at each end of the board, then knit the middle pegs.

Stocking stitch produces a very tight weave

Rib Stitch

Woven on the board and similar to the Stocking Cast On, except Rib is worked at a slight angle.
Note: you must cast on with an even number of pegs.

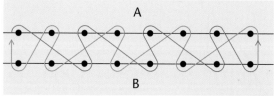

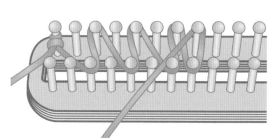

Start at 1A, down to peg 3B, up to peg 3A, down to peg 5B, then up to 5A. Continue weaving your yarn, skipping every other peg. You will be wrapping at a slight angle. When you reach the end of the board wrap the lower and upper pegs directly across from each other. Turn your board around and cover all the pegs that you skipped to complete a circular.

Knit Over Process: First knit the first 2 sets of pegs at each end of the board, then knit the middle pegs. Repeat.

Rib Stitch has the rib look on both sides. Like regular needle ribbing, the ribbing on the board can be used for cuffs where you would want a snugger fit.

Simple Stitch

Simple Stitch provides an open weave, perfect for thick yarns. Also known as the Zigzag Stitch and the Fashion Stitch, in the Simple Stitch, a circular is completed in one pass down the board.

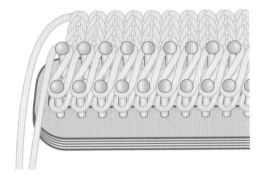

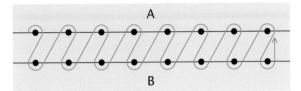

Start at peg 1A, down to peg 1B, then up to 2A, then down to 2B. Continue along the board, covering all the pegs. The yarn will be towards the outside of each peg.

Next row: Wrap the opposite peg, continue wrapping across the board. Be sure to wrap the pegs in the same direction as the previous row.

Note: The first peg is not wrapped; it becomes a turning peg.

Knit Over Process: Knit over all down one side; then knit over the other side. Knit over on the last peg you wrapped first to anchor the yarn.

Note: Always start knitting over on the same side. Repeat.

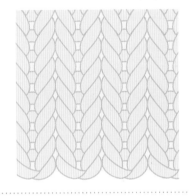

Figure 8 Stitch

The Figure 8 Stitch is a very open, airy stitch, perfect to use with novelty yarns and super bulky yarns.

It allows the yarns to 'fluff' and look their best. The Figure 8 Stitch is also used to cast on extra stitches at the beginning or end of the board.

Start at peg 1A, go around it, towards the outside of the loom. Take it down to peg 1B with yarn between peg 1B and peg 2B, wrap around the peg, then go up to peg 2A, between peg 2A and peg 3A, wrap around peg 2A, then go down to peg 2B. Continue to the end of the board. Repeat the same weaving for the next rows.

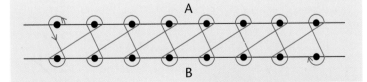

Knitting Over Process

Knit over on one side of the board, then knit over on the opposite side. Always start knitting over on the same side.

TIP

Place a stitch marker or a contrasting piece of yarn on the side that you need to knit over first.

Colour Changes

Changing the yarn colour every few rows will give horizontal stripes, and is a great way to use up oddments of yarn from your stash.

Horizontal Stripes

Creating horizontal stripes is the easiest way to give your knits a fresh look. Always change yarns at the beginning of a row. To attach the new colour/skein, leave a 12.5–20cm (5–8in) beginning tail.

Insert the beginning tail of the new yarn through one of the stitches in the centre of the board. Lay the two ends in the centre – the ends will be hidden between the knitting.

Wrap with the new colour/skein down the board in the established pattern.

Vertical Stripes

These are created by using the Simple Stitch or the figure 8 stitch. Locate the area where you want the stripes to begin. Insert the beginning tail end through one of the stitches in the centre of the board. Lay the tail end in the centre of the board; once you start weaving and knitting, the tail end will be hidden.

Since you will be dealing with two strands of yarn within the same row, you need to do the wrapping in two steps. Pick up the main colour yarn (MC) and wrap all the pegs desired in that colour. Be sure to wrap it in sets (1A, 1B, 2A, 2B, and so on). At the end of the row, drop the MC. Go back to the beginning of the row, pick up the contrasting colour (CC) and wrap the pegs skipped. The unused colour will run from peg to peg. Knit over as usual. Continue wrapping in the established pattern.

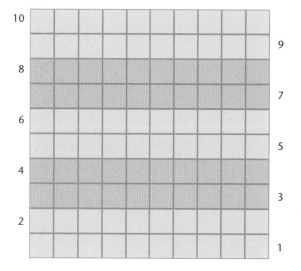

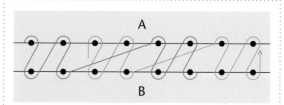

Checkerboard Pattern

To change the colours around to create a checkerboard pattern, change the wrapping process: wrap the pegs that were wrapped with MC with CC, and vice versa.

Shaping

Increasing and decreasing on a knitting board is similar to shaping in the round. Two methods are demonstrated below. Make sure you have only one loop on each peg to start.

Increasing Method 1

Method 1 – recommended for when casting on more than 2 stitches.

Inc1: To increase the number of stitches, simply figure-8 wrap the next set of empty pegs twice. Wrap the other pegs so that the entire board has 2 loops on each peg. Knit over as usual. For example, the knitting board below has stitches from pegs

2–7. Increase at peg 8 by figure-8 wrapping peg 8A and 8B twice. Increase on the other side by figure-8 wrapping peg 1A and 1B twice.

This type of increase method leaves a step edge. For a gradual increase, try the next method.

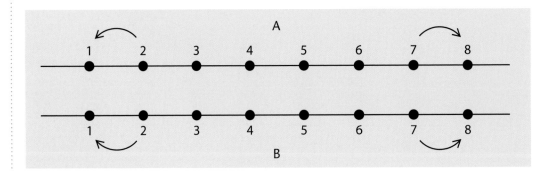

Increasing Method 2

Make 1 – recommended for when increasing only 2 stitches at a time.

The Make 1 (M1) increase method is completed within a row. It provides a gradual increase that leaves a clean angled edge.

Move the last set of stitches outwards to the next set of empty pegs. You have created an empty set of pegs. With your knitting tool or crochet hook, reach in and pick the running strand from one peg to the next, twist it and place it on one of the empty pegs. Reach for the strand on the other side, twist it and place it on the other empty peg. Wrap your board as usual; all pegs should have 2 loops on them. Knit over as usual.

For example, assume you have stitches from pegs 2–7. Move the stitches from pegs 7A and 7B to the empty pegs 8A and 8B. You have created an empty set of pegs and increased by 1 stitch. Reach for the ladder going to peg 8A, twist it and place it on empty peg 7A. Reach for the ladder going to peg 8B, twist it and place it on empty peg 7B.

You can also create an empty set of pegs other than at the end of the board. Just move all the stitches one space over, leaving an empty space where you want the increase to happen. To create a less noticeable increase, only increase every 3–4 rows.

Decreasing Method 1

Use this at the very end/beginning of a row.

Dec: The decrease is similar to the increase method with the exception that the stitches need to move towards the centre of the board. The pegs adjacent to the decrease will have an extra stitch.

1 Move the last stitches inwards to the adjacent peg.
2 Wrap and knit over. Make sure to knit over 2 over 1 on the pegs with the extra stitches.

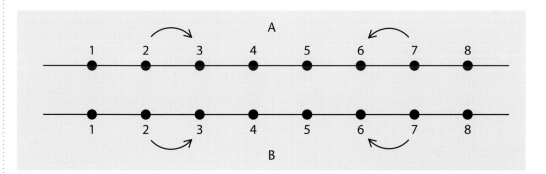

Decreasing Method 2

Use this within the row: it creates a more gradual decrease.

Let's assume you have all the pegs covered as in the diagram above. You want to decrease by 2 stitches at each end.

K2tog: Move the stitches from pegs 7A and 7B to pegs 6A and 6B. Move the stitches from pegs 8A and 8B to pegs 7A and 7B – one decrease done on the right side of the loom. Wrap the board as called for in the pattern and knit over as usual. When you reach the pegs with 3 loops on them, knit over the bottommost 2 stitches. Pegs 8A and 8B are empty.

I recommend Method 2 for most decreases as it leaves a less noticeable decrease angle. To make it more subtle, only decrease every 3–4 rows.

Finishing Techniques

Casting off and finishing your work on a board loom is similar to working in the round.
A few more techniques become possible.

Casting Off on a Board

You will need a crochet hook that works with the yarn for the project. Each peg must have only 1 loop. Cut the working yarn, leaving a 15cm (6in) tail. Begin on the opposite side from where the yarn tail is located.

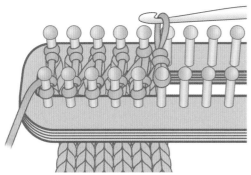

1 With a crochet hook, remove the loop from peg 1B, leave it on the crochet hook. Remove the loop from peg 1A, place it on the crochet hook. Remove the loop from peg 2A, place it on the hook. The crochet hook should have 3 loops on it.

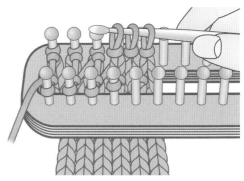

2 Pull the last 2 stitches added through the back stitch; 1 stitch remains on the crochet hook.

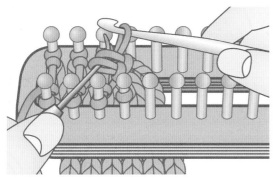

3 Remove the loop from peg 2A, place it on the crochet hook. Remove the loop from peg 3B, place it on the crochet hook. Crochet hook has 3 loops again. Pull the last 2 stitches added through the back stitch; 1 stitch remains on crochet hook.

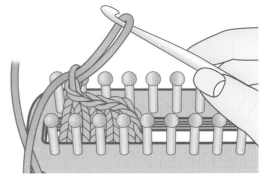

4 Repeat until you reach the end of the board and all the stitches have been removed. Catch the tail end and hook through the last loop on the crochet hook. Tighten and weave in the ends.

Finishing Off the Cast On Edge

The anchor yarn is holding the first cast on loops as 'live' stitches. When the project is completed, the cast-on edge needs to be finished by crocheting.

The following steps will show how to accomplish this essential part of the knitted garment. In order to finish the 'live' stitches, you need to have a crochet hook that will work with the weight of yarn used.

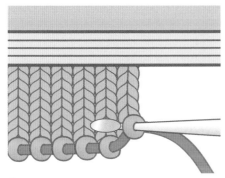

1 Insert crochet hook in the first stitch.

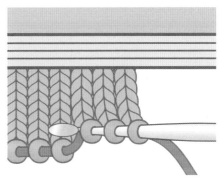

2 Insert the hook through the next 2 stitches.

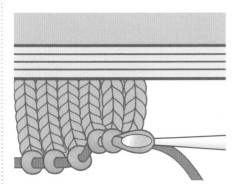

3 Pass the stitch on the front of the hook through the middle stitch, and then pass it through the back stitch, leaving only 1 loop on the hook.

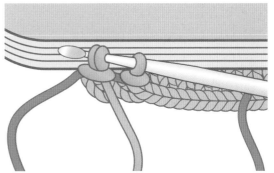

4 Repeat steps 2 and 3 with the remaining stitches. When you reach the end, form a chain with the yarn tail end and pass it through the last loop. After all the stitches have been cast off with the crochet hook, you can remove the anchor yarn by pulling it out.

The Patterns

Circular Patterns

Work in the round on a circular loom with this exciting selection of patterns.

84 Simple Hat

85 Garter Stitch Hat

86 Peek-a-Boo Slouch Hat

88 Winter Hat

90 I-Cord Hot Pad

91 Baby Cocoon Set

94 Child's Mock Cable Hat

95 Child's Earflap Hat

98 Ribbed Leg Warmers

Sock Patterns

Nothing beats a pair of handmade socks!

100 Chunky Ribbed Socks

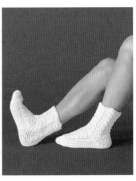
102 Mock Cable Socks

104 Weekend Socks

Flat Panel Patterns

Flat panels can be transformed into a wide range of different garments and accessories.

108 Trendy Scarf

109 Urban Chic Cowl

110 Garter Stitch Scarf

111 Fingerless Mitts

112 Cowl

113 Rainbow Fish Pillow

114 Brocade Baby Sweater

117 Soft Blanket and Hat

118 Bliss Baby Blanket

120 Mock Cables Poncho

122 Ruana

126 Waves Shrug

128 Glasses Case

Board Patterns

Work these patterns on a knitting board for double-knit, reversible designs.

130 Power Pink Scarf

131 Scarflet

132 Double Knit Ribbed Scarf

133 Striped Scarf

134 Rosy Berry Throw

Felted Patterns

Create a firm fabric by knitting and then felting these great projects.

138 Yoga Mat Bag

139 Felted Accessories Clutch

140 Felted Handbag

142 Felted Laptop Cosy

144 Soft Felt Slippers

Circular Patterns

Now you have mastered the basic skills of loom
knitting, here are some patterns for you to try out.
The following are all worked in the round.

Simple Hat

Let's kick things off with a basic hat pattern, using what we have learned so far.

MATERIALS

Knitting Loom

40 (36) peg large gauge round loom; adult (child)

Yarn

46m (50yd) of bulky weight yarn [Rowan Big Wool, Lucky, 100% wool, 79m (87yd) per 100g (3½oz) ball used in sample]

Tools

Knitting tool
Tapestry needle

Size

Heads up to 51cm (20in) circumference

Tension

4 stitches and 7 rows to 5cm (2in) over Pattern Stitch

TIP

If you don't have any bulky weight yarn, use 2 strands of aran weight/medium weight yarn and treat it as one strand of bulky yarn, then check your tension.

Pattern notes

Worked in the round using Single Stitch (see page 32).

Hat Brim

Cast on with the E-Wrap cast on method (see page 30).
Knit 1 row of Chunky Braid Stitch (see page 34).

Hat Body

Knit in Single Stitch until item measures 18cm (7in) from cast on edge.

Crown of Hat

Decrease for the crown as follows: Move the loop from every even peg number to its neighbouring peg to the right (loop from peg 2 to peg 1, loop from peg 4 to peg 3, etc). Odd pegs have two loops, even numbered pegs are empty. In Single Stitch, knit over 2 over 1 on all pegs with stitches on them.

Cast off using the Gather Cast Off method (see page 35). Weave in all yarn tail ends.

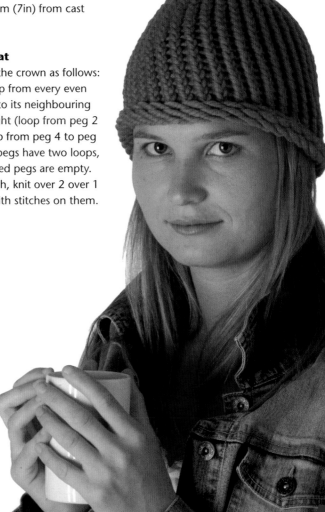

Garter Stitch Hat

This simple hat has a scarf and mittens to match on pages 110 and 111 – knit them as a set for a perfect quick-knit gift.

MATERIALS

Knitting Loom

40 peg large gauge round loom

Yarn

64m (70yd) of super bulky weight yarn [Rowan Big Wool, 100% wool, 79m (87yd) per 100g (3½oz) ball, Bohemian used in sample]

Tools

Knitting tool
Stitch holder
Tapestry needle

Size

Heads up to 51cm (20in) circumference

Tension

8 sts and 12 rows to 10cm (4in)

Pattern notes

Worked in the round using Knit Stitch (see page 44) and Purl Stitch (see page 45)

Note: If you would like to knit this hat and have a looser fit, work it in Single Stitch instead.

Hat Body

Cast on using the Chain Cast On method (see page 43).

Rnd 1: Knit.
Rnd 2: Purl.
Repeat rows 1–2 until hat measures 20cm (8in) from cast on edge.

Crown Decreases

Divide the stitches on the loom into 4 groups of 10 stitches. Each group will be worked separately.

Row 1: Move the first stitch at each end of the first wedge over to the 2nd peg (peg 1 to peg 2; peg 10 to peg 9). Knit all the stitches. Knit 2 over 1 on the end pegs.
Row 2: Purl.
Repeat rows 1–2 until you have only 2 stitches left on the wedge. Break the yarn leaving a 36cm (14in) tail. Place the last stitch remaining from the wedge on a stitch holder.

Attach yarn at the first peg of the next wedge to be worked and repeat wedge instructions.

Closing the Crown

Seam the sides using the yarn tail end from each of the wedges using Mattress Stitch (see page 51).

Cast Off

Once all the sides have been seamed, thread the tapestry needle with yarn and pass it through the four stitches on the stitch holder, cinch it closed with the Gather Cast Off method (see page 35). Pass the needle to the reverse side of the hat and weave in yarn ends.

Peek-a-Boo Slouch Hat

A play with colours with this double layer slouchy hat. The lace layer allows for the bottom layer's colour to show through for a peek-a-boo effect.

MATERIALS

Knitting Loom

104 peg regular gauge round loom.

Yarn

274m (300yd) DK merino/silk blend yarn [Manos del Uruguay Silk Blend Yarn, merino silk blend, 137m (150yd) per 50g (1¾oz) skein used in sample]

Tools

Knitting tool
Tapestry needle

Other materials

2.5 cm (1in) button (optional)

Size

Heads up to 51cm (20in) circumference

Tension

24 stitches and 30 rows to 10cm (4in)

Pattern notes

This hat was worked on the All-n-One knitting loom, an adjustable knitting loom, which is recommended to allow for the crown decrease. The hat is worked in two layers, a bottom layer worked in a contrast colour (CC) and a top layer worked in the main colour (MC). The two layers are then seamed together.

Abbreviations

k = Knit Stitch
k2tog = knit 2 stitches together
p = Purl Stitch
sts = stitches
sl = slip (skip the peg with the working yarn behind the peg)
ssk = Slip, Slip, Knit
rnd(s) = round(s)
rep = repeat
yo = yarn over (e-wrap the peg, on the next row/round, undo the E-Wrap and lay the strand of yarn in front of the peg).

Bottom layer

Cast on 104 sts, prepare to work in the rnd.

Rnds 1–7: *k2, p2; rep from * to the end of rnd.

Rnd 8: p to end of rnd.

Rnd 9: k to the end of rnd.

Rep Rnd 9: until item measures 20 cm (8 in) from cast on edge.

**Crown Decreases

Move all sts to a piece of scrap yarn. Set knitting loom to 52 pegs. Place sts back on the knitting loom, 2 sts per peg.

Next rnd: k to end of rnd (treat both sts on pegs as if they were one st).

Move all sts to a piece of scrap yarn. Set knitting loom to 26 pegs. Place sts back on the loom, 2 sts per peg.

Next rnd: k to end of rnd (treat both sts on pegs as if they were one st). Remove with Gather Cast Off (see page 35).

Weave ends in. Block lightly.**

Top layer

Leaving a 50cm (20in) beginning yarn tail, cast on 104 sts, and prepare to work in the rnd.

Prep row: k to end of rnd.

Rnd 1: *k1, k2tog, k1 [yo, k1] twice, ssk; rep from * to end.

Rnd 2: k to end of rnd.

Rnd 3: *k1, k2tog, yo, k3, yo, ssk; rep from * to end.

Rnd 4: k to end of rnd.

Rnd 5: *k1, yo, k1, ssk, k1, k2tog, k1, yo; rep from * to end.

Rnd 6: k to end of rnd.

Rnd 7: *k2, yo, ssk, k1, k2tog, yo, k1; rep from * to end.

Rnd 8: k to end of rnd.

Rep Rnds 1–8: until item measures 20cm (8in) from cast on edge. Work from ** to ** of crown decreases from bottom layer.

Assembly

Use the beginning yarn tail coming from the top layer to seam the top layer to the bottom layer as follows: line up the Cast On round of the top layer to the Purl round (rnd 8) of the bottom layer and use either an Overcast Stitch or Mattress Stitch (see page 51) to join both layers together. Weave ends in. Block again if necessary.

Top Layer Stitch Breakdown

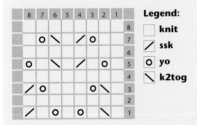

Legend:
- ☐ knit
- ╱ ssk
- ○ yo
- ╲ k2tog

Repeat the following instructions every 8 pegs.

Rnd 1: K1, k2tog, k1, [yo, k1] twice, ssk.

Take loop off peg 2 and hold it. Move loop from peg 3 to peg 2. Place held loop back on peg 2 (two loops on peg 2). Move loop from peg 4 to peg 3 (peg 4 is empty). Take loop off peg 8 and hold it. Move loop from peg 7 to peg 8. Place held loop back on peg 8 (two loops on peg 8).

Move loop from peg 6 to peg 7 (peg 6 is empty).

Knit to end of row, treating two loops as one on pegs 2 and 8, and E-Wrapping empty pegs 4 and 6.

Rnd 2, 4, 6, 8: K to end of rnd.

Rnd 3: K1, k2tog, yo, k3, yo, ssk.

Take loop off peg 2 and hold it. Move loop from peg 3 to peg 2. Place held loop back on peg 2 (two loops on peg 2; peg 3 is empty).

Take loop off peg 8 and hold it. Move loop from peg 7 to peg 8. Place held loop back on peg 8 (two loops on peg 8; peg 7 is empty).

Knit to end of row, treating two loops as one on pegs 2 and 8, and E-Wrapping empty pegs 3 and 7.

Rnd 5: K1, yo, k1, ssk, k1, k2tog, yo, k1.

Take loop off peg 4 and hold it. Move loop from peg 3 to peg 4. Place held loop back on peg 4 (two loops on peg 4).

Move loop from peg 2 to peg 3 (peg 2 is empty).

Take loop off peg 6 and hold it. Move loop from peg 7 to peg 6. Place held loop back on peg 6 (two loops on peg 6).

Move loop from peg 8 to peg 7 (peg 8 is empty).

Knit to end of row, treating two loops as one on pegs 4 and 6, and E-Wrapping empty pegs 2 and 8.

Rnd 7: K2, yo, k2tog, k1, ssk, yo, k1

Take loop off peg 4 and hold it. Move loop from peg 3 to peg 4. Place held loop back on peg 4 (two loops on peg 4; peg 3 is empty).

Take loop off peg 6 and hold it. Move loop from peg 7 to peg 6. Place held loop back on peg 6 (two loops on peg 6; peg 7 is empty).

Knit to end of row, treating two loops as one on pegs 4 and 6, and E-Wrapping empty pegs 3 and 7.

Winter Hat

The beauty of stranded knitting comes alive with this wintery hat. It depicts a landscape of falling snowflakes. Knitted with a classic, soft merino wool, this hat is sure to keep you warm during the winter months.

MATERIALS

Knitting Loom

60 peg regular gauge round loom

Yarn

183m (200yd) main colour (MC); 46m (50yd) contrast colour (CC) [Patons Classic Merino Wool, 100% Wool, 204m (223yd) per 100g (3½oz) ball used in sample]

Tools

Knitting tool
Tapestry needle
5 stitch markers
Row counter (optional)

Size

Heads up to 53cm (21in) circumference

Tension

13 sts and 20 rows to 10cm (4in)

Pattern notes
Use 2 strands of yarn throughout.

Abbreviations
MC = main colour
CC = contrasting colour
k = Knit Stitch
p = Purl Stitch
rnd = round

Snowflake Stitch Pattern
Multiple of 12

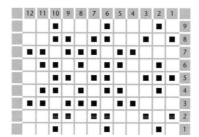

Key
☐ Main Colour
■ Contrasting Colour

Instructions
Place stitch markers 12 pegs apart. Cast on 60 sts in the round with Chain Cast On method (see page 43) and MC.

Rnd 1: *K2, p2; rep from * to the end of round.
Repeat rnd 1 until brim measures 5cm (2in) from cast on edge.

Knit the 9 rows from chart as follows:
Rnd 1: *K1 with MC, knit 1 with CC, k3 with MC, k1 with CC, k3 with MC, k1 with CC, k2 with MC; rep from * to the end of round.

Rnd 2: *K1 with CC, k1 with MC, k1 with CC, k2 with MC, k2 with CC, k1 with MC, knit 2 with CC, k2 with MC; rep from * to end.
Rnd 3: *K3 with MC, k2 with CC, k1 with MC, k3 with CC, k1 with MC, k2 with CC; rep from * to end.
Rnd 4: *K1 with MC, k1 with CC, k2 with MC, k2 with CC, k1 with MC, k1 with CC, k1 with MC, k2 with CC, k1 with MC; rep from * to end.
Rnd 5: *K3 with CC, k2 with MC, k2 with CC, k1 with MC, k2 with CC, k2 with MC; rep from * to end.
Rnd 6: *K1 with MC, k1 with CC, k2 with MC, k2 with CC, k1 with MC, k1 with CC, k1 with MC, k2 with CC, k1 with MC; rep from * to the end of round.
Rnd 7: *K3 with MC, k2 with CC, k1 with MC, k3 with CC, k1 with MC, k2 with CC; rep from * to end of round.
Rnd 8: *K1 with CC, k1 with MC, k1 with CC, k2 with MC, k2 with CC, k1 with MC, k2 with CC, k2 with MC; rep from * to the end of round.
Rnd 9: *K1 with MC, k1 with CC, k3 with MC, k1 with CC, k3 with MC, k1 with CC, k2 with MC; rep from * to the end of round.

Knit in Stocking Stitch for 10cm (4in).

Cast off using the Gather Cast Off method (see page 35).

I-Cord Hot Pad

Making I-cords is seriously addictive. Once you have got the bug, you will have to find something to do with all those cords! Here's one idea; you are sure to have more.

MATERIALS

Knitting Loom

Large gauge round loom with at least 3 pegs

Yarn

40yd (36.5m) bulky weight yarn [Manos Del Uruguay, hand-spun 100% wool, 125m (137yd) per 100g (3½oz) skein used in sample]

Tools

Knitting tool
Tapestry needle

Instructions

Make a 92cm (3ft) long I-cord (see page 39) and fasten off. Place the cord on a flat surface and coil it around in a circle. Sew the I-cord sides together with the same yarn and a tapestry needle.

Start at the centre on the back and work to the end, weaving in any yarn ends, to make a woolly mat. Wool is naturally heat-resistant and washable and so is hygenic for use in the kitchen.

TIP

This project uses the 3-stitch I-cord. To make a thicker or thinner I-cord, simply cast on additional or fewer stitches.

Baby Cocoon Set

Swaddle your precious little one in this adorable baby bunting, providing them with a feeling of security and love.

MATERIALS

Knitting Loom

At least 90 (102) peg regular gauge All-n-One adjustable loom.

Yarn

320m (350yd) aran weight merino wool yarn [Knit Picks Preciosa Tonal, Blue Skies (100% merino wool), 250m (273yd) per 100g (3½oz) used in sample]

Tools

Knitting tool
Tapestry needle

Measurements

Newborn–3 months:
45cm (18in) circumference, 50cm (20in) long
3–6 months: 45cm (20in) circumference, 55cm (22in) long

Tension

19 sts and 32 rows to 10cm (4in)

Pattern notes

Hat and Cocoon were worked on All-n-One knitting loom, an adjustable knitting loom, which is recommended to allow for the crown decrease on the hat. The Cocoon has a small hood shaped with short rows. If the hood is not desired, you can omit it.

Abbreviations

Approx = approximately
k = Knit Stitch
k2tog = knit 2 stitches together
p = Purl Stitch
sts = stitches
ssk = Slip, Slip, Knit
rnd(s) = round(s)
rep = repeat
yo = yarn over (E-Wrap the peg, on the next row/round, undo the E-Wrap and lay the strand of yarn in front of the peg)
W&T = wrap and turn. Remove loop from peg, E-Wrap peg, place loop back on the peg.

Hat

Set knitting loom at 60 (66 pegs). Cast on 60 (66) sts, prepare to work in the rnd.
Newborn–3 months:
Rnds 1–8: *k2, p2; rep from * to end of rnd.
3–6 months:
Rnds 1–8: *k1, p1; rep from * to end of rnd.
All sizes:
Rnd 9: k to end of rnd.
Rnd 10: *yo, ssk, k1, k2tog, yo, k1; rep from * to end of rnd.

Rnd 11: k to end of rnd.
Rnd 12: *k1, yo, k3tog, yo, k2; rep from * to end of rnd.
Rnd 13: k to end of rnd.
Rep Rnds 10–13: 11 (12) times, or until desired length.

Crown Decreases

Move all sts to a piece of scrap yarn. Set knitting loom to 30 (32) pegs. Place sts back on the knitting loom, 2 sts per peg (larger size, you will have one peg with 3 sts).
Next rnd: k to end of rnd (treat both sts on peg as if one st). Move all sts to a piece of scrap yarn. Use Gather Cast Off (see page 35). Weave ends in. Block lightly.

Cocoon

Set knitting loom to 90 (102) pegs.

Rnds 1–25: k to the end of rnd.

Rnd 26: *yo, ssk, k1, k2tog, yo, k1; rep from * to end of rnd.

Rnd 27: k to the end of rnd.

Rnd 28: *k1, yo, k3tog, yo, k2; rep from * to end of rnd.

Rnd 29: k to the end of rnd.

Rep rnds 10–13 until panel measures approx 43 (48) cm (17 (19) in) from cast on edge (end on rnd 29).

Creating the Hood – the hood is created by working short rows over half the sts.

Next row: k from peg 1–49. W&T on peg 50.

Next row: k from peg 49 to peg 2. W&T peg 1.

Next row: k from peg 2 to peg 48. W&T peg 49.

Next row: k from peg 48 to peg 3. W&T peg 2.

Next row: k from peg 3 to peg 47. W&T peg 48.

Next row: k from peg 47 to peg 4. W&T peg 3.

Next row: k from peg 4 to peg 46. W&T peg 47.

Next row: k from peg 46 to peg 5. W&T peg 4.

Next row: k from peg 5 to peg 45. W&T peg 46.

Next row: k from peg 45 to peg 6. W&T peg 5.

Next row: k from peg 6 to peg 44. W&T peg 45.

Next row: k from peg 44 to peg 7. W&T peg 6.

Next row: k from peg 7 to peg 43. W&T peg 44.

Next row: k from peg 43 to peg 8. W&T peg 7.

Next row: k from peg 8 to peg 42. W&T peg 43.

Next row: k from peg 42 to peg 9. W&T peg 8.

Next row: k from peg 9 to peg 41. W&T peg 42.

Next row: k from peg 41 to peg 10. W&T peg 9.

Next row: k from peg 10 to peg 40. W&T peg 41.

Next row: k from peg 40 to peg 11. W&T peg 10.

Next row: k from peg 11 to peg 39. W&T peg 40.

Next row: k from peg 39 to peg 11. W&T peg 10 (lift both loops on peg with 2 loops on it).

Next row: k from peg 11 to peg 40. W&T peg 41 (lift both loops on peg with 2 loops on it).

Next row: k from peg 40 to peg 10. W&T peg 9 (lift all loops on peg with 3 loops on it).

Next row: k from peg 10 to peg 41. W&T peg 42 (lift all loops on peg with 3 loops on it).

Next row: k from peg 41 to peg 9. W&T peg 8 (lift all loops on peg with 3 loops on it).

Next row: k from peg 9 to peg 42. W&T peg 43 (lift all loops on peg with 3 loops on it).

Next row: k from peg 42 to peg 8. W&T peg 7 (lift all loops on peg with 3 loops on it).

Next row: k from peg 8 to peg 43. W&T peg 44 (lift all loops on peg with 3 loops on it).

Next row: k from peg 43 to peg 7. W&T peg 6 (lift all loops on peg with 3 loops on it).

Next row: k from peg 7 to peg 44. W&T peg 45 (lift all loops on peg with 3 loops on it).

Next row: k from peg 44 to peg 6. W&T peg 5 (lift all loops on peg with 3 loops on it).

Next row: k from peg 6 to peg 45. W&T peg 46 (lift all loops on peg with 3 loops on it).

Next row: k from peg 45 to peg 5. W&T peg 4 (lift all loops on peg with 3 loops on it).

Next row: k from peg 5 to peg 46. W&T peg 47 (lift all loops on peg with 3 loops on it).

Next row: k from peg 46 to peg 4. W&T peg 3 (lift all loops on peg with 3 loops on it).

Next row: k from peg 4 to peg 47. W&T peg 48 (lift all loops on peg with 3 loops on it).

Next row: k from peg 47 to peg 3. W&T peg 2 (lift all loops on peg with 3 loops on it).

Next row: k from peg 3 to peg 48. W&T peg 49 (lift all loops on peg with 3 loops on it).

Next row: k from peg 48 to peg 2. W&T peg 1 (lift all loops on peg with 3 loops on it).

Next row: k from peg 2 to 49. W&T peg 50 (lift all loops on peg with 3 loops on it).

Continue working in the round from this point forwards.

Next rnd: k to the end of rnd (treat the pegs with two loops on as one loop).

Next rnd: p to the end of rnd.

Next rnd: k to the end of rnd.

Next rnd: p to the end of rnd.

Next rnd. K to the end of rnd.

Cast off loosely with Basic Cast Off method (see page 35). Weave ends in. Block.

Note: it is important not to let babies get too hot, so make sure this cosy set is only used in appropriate conditions.

Child's Mock Cable Hat

Learn the basics of crossing stitches while creating a classic hat. Choose some pretty colours and knit a hat in each one.

MATERIALS

Knitting Loom

36 peg large gauge round loom

Yarn

46 m (50 yd) bulky weight yarn [GGH Aspen, 50% fine merino wool 50% microfibre, 57 m (63 yd) per 50 g (1¾ oz) used in sample]

Tools

Knitting tool
Tapestry needle

Sizes

Child, head approximately 39.5cm (15½in) circumference

Tension

10 stitches and 14 rows to 10cm (4in)

Pattern Notes

Knitted in the round.

Abbreviations

TW = twist right (take the loops off pegs A & B, place stitch from peg A on peg B, place stitch from peg B on peg A). Knit them.
p2tog = A decrease row – combine the two Purl Stitches into one stitch by moving the stitch from the peg on the left to the peg on the right. (See page 58.)

Cable Twist Rib Pattern

Multiple of 4 stitches:
Round 1, 2, 4: P2, k2.
Round 3: P2, TW

Stitch Pattern Chart

4	3	2	1	
			•	•	4
/	/	•	•	3
			•	•	2
			•	•	1

Chart Key
K Knit |
P Purl •
TW Twist /

Instructions

Cast on 36 sts, prepare to work in the round.

Round 1, 2, 4: *P2, k2; rep from * to end of round.
Round 3: *P2, TW; rep from * to end of round.
Rep rounds 1–4, 7 times

Crown Shaping

*P2tog, k2; rep from * to end of round.

Cast off with Gather Cast Off method (see page 35).

Child's Earflap Hat

The perfect child's hat – it will keep your little one's ears warm. Experiment with different colour stripes, or alternative stitches to make pattern variations – perfect to show school or team spirit.

MATERIALS

Knitting Loom

36 peg large gauge round loom

Yarn

64m (70yd) bulky weight yarn

- Striped version: 46m (50yd) main colour (MC), 18m (20yd) contrast colour (CC) [Rowan Big Wool (100% Merino wool, 80m (87yd) per 100g (3½oz) ball in Bohemian (CC) and Black (MC) used in sample.]

- Solid version: 64m (70yd) [Encore Mega Colourspun in colour 7130 super bulky, 75% acrylic, 25% wool, 59m (64yd) per 100g (3½oz) used in sample.]

Tools

Knitting tool
Stitch holder
Tapestry needle

Size

Child, head approximately 38cm (15in) circumference

Tension

5 sts and 8 rows to 5cm (2in)

Pattern notes

When the pattern states, 'using X colour yarn', simply pick up the yarn colour needed and start wrapping. Pattern is knit in the round, with the exception of the earflaps.

Solid Colour Version: Use the same bulky colour yarn throughout, omitting the colour changes.

Abbreviations

k = Knit Stitch
k2tog = knit 2 stitches together
sts = stitches
ssk = Slip, Slip, Knit
MC = main colour
CC = contrasting colour

Decrease Row: K1, k2tog, knit to last 3 sts, ssk, k1.

Earflap Instructions

Make 2
Knitted as flat panels (see page 54) in Garter Stitch (see page 46).

Instructions

Using CC cast on 8 stitches.
Row 1, 3, 5, 7: Purl.
Row 2, 4, 6: Knit.
Row 8: Decrease Row (6 sts left).
Row 9, 11, 13: Purl.
Row 10, 12: Knit.
Row 14: Decrease row (4 sts).
Row 15, 17: Purl.
Row 16: Knit.
Row 18: Decrease Row (2 sts).
Row 19: Purl.

Row 20 and on: Using the 2 sts remaining on the loom knit a 2-stitch I-cord (see page 39), 38cm (15in) long.
Cast off. Weave in all yarn tail ends. Earflaps completed. Set aside.

Hat Body

Knitted in the round.
Cast on all pegs using MC and the Chain Cast On method (see page 43).

Hat Brim

Knitted in garter stitch as follows:
Row 1, 3, 5: Purl.
Row 2, 4, 6: Knit.
Attach CC at peg 1.

Attach Earflaps

Pick up 7 stitches from the earflaps' cast on edge and place them on the following pegs – on top of the loops already on the pegs:
Earflap 1: Place on pegs 1–7.
Earflap 2: Place on pegs 19–25.

Continue knitting body of the hat:
Row 7–8: Using CC knit 2 rows. On Row 7, make sure to knit 2 over 1 on pegs 1–7, and 19–25. Cut CC.
Row 9–20: Using MC: Knit 12 rows.
Row 21–23: Attach CC: Knit 3 rows with CC.
Row 24: Knit 1 row in MC.
Row 25–27: Knit 3 rows in CC.
Row 28–30: Knit 3 rows in MC.

(continued on next page)

TIP

To decrease the crown of the hat, knit it in flat panels. Divide the number of the pegs used into wedges that contain the same number of stitches. Work each wedge as a flat panel and decrease each flat panel to make a triangle. At the end, seam the wedges with an invisible stitch such as Mattress Stitch (see page 51).

Crown of Hat

The crown of the hat is worked in four wedges of nine stitches each and later seamed together.

Special Instructions:

Decrease Row: K1, k2tog, knit to last 3 sts, ssk, k1.

Knit wedges as follows:
Row 1, 3, 5, 7, 9: Knit.
Row 2, 4, 6, 8: Decrease row – follow special instructions above. Place the last stitch on a stitch holder. Cut yarn and attach the yarn to the next wedge.

Wedge 1 (pegs 1–9).
Wedge 2 (pegs 10–18).
Wedge 3 (pegs 19–27).
Wedge 4 (pegs 28–36).
Seam the wedges together using Mattress Stitch (see page 51).

Place the 4 stitches from the stitch holder back onto the knitting loom, 2 stitches on peg 1 and 2 stitches on peg 2.
Knit a 6–inch, 2 stitch I-cord. Cast off the I-cord and form a small knot with the I-cord to make a bobble.

Turn hat inside out and weave in all the yarn ends, making sure to cross the yarns where the colour changes occurred to prevent any holes.

Ribbed Leg Warmers

These leg warmers are snug and comfortable to wear, worked in Rib Stitch to provide a stretchy fit. Wear them over trousers or with a skirt to keep your legs cosy.

MATERIALS

Knitting Loom

24 peg large gauge round loom

Yarn

Approximately 165m (180yd) of bulky weight yarn [Crystal Palace Iceland, colour 7256, 100% Wool, 99m (109yd) per 100g (3½oz) ball used in sample]

Tools

Knitting tool
Tapestry needle

Size

56cm (22in) long

Tension

6 sts and 8 rows to 5cm (2in) over Rib Stitch

Pattern notes
Knitted in the round using all the pegs on the loom.

Abbreviations
k = Knit Stitch
p = Purl Stitch

Stitch Pattern
K2, P2, repeat from * to * to the end of the round.

Instructions
(Make 2)
Cast on with the E-Wrap
Cast On method (see page 30).

Round 1: *K2, p2*, repeat from * to * to the end of the round. Continue in pattern until item measures 56cm (22in) from cast on edge.

Cast off using the Single Crochet Cast Off method (see page 48).

TIP
The cast on and cast off need to be done loosely or they will be tight around the legs.

Sock patterns

There is something so fulfilling about opening a sock drawer and seeing rows of hand-knitted goodness. Try out these patterns to get started on the sock knitting journey: you will soon be designing your own.

Chunky Ribbed Socks

An easy introduction to socks – the stretchy ribs make them a perfect fit for almost every adult. Knitted with alpaca yarn for a most luxurious pair of socks.

MATERIALS

Knitting Loom

24 peg large gauge round loom

Yarn

137m (150yd) bulky yarn [Ultra Alpaca Berroco 50% alpaca, 50% wool, 197m (215yd) per 100g (3½oz) ball used in sample]

Tools

Knitting tool
Tapestry needle
2.5mm (US size 8) double-pointed knitting needles for grafting

Size

Adult (foot length adjustable in pattern)

Tension

9 sts and 14 rows to 10cm (4in)

Abbreviations

k = Knit Stitch
p = Purl Stitch
W&T = wrap and turn. Remove loop from peg, E-Wrap peg, place loop back on the peg. Knit back in the opposite direction.

Instructions

Work sock leg
Cast on in the round with the Cable Cast On method (see page 42).

Rnd 1: P1, *k4, p2; rep from * to the last 5 sts, k4, p1.
Rep rnd 1 until leg measures 15cm (6in) from cast on edge.

Working the Short-row Heel

Note: The heel is worked as a flat panel. The cup for the heel is formed by knitting short rows. Remember to wrap each of the turning pegs.

Row 1: K11 (from peg 1–11), W&T peg 12.
Row 2: K10 (from peg 11–2), W&T peg 1.
Row 3: K9 (from peg 2–10), W&T peg 11.
Row 4: K8 (from peg 10–3), W&T peg 2.
Row 5: K7 (from peg 3–9), W&T peg 10.
Row 6: K6 (from peg 9–4), W&T peg 3.
Row 7: K5 (from peg 4–8), W&T peg 9.
Row 8: K4 (from peg 8–5), W&T peg 4.

Row 9: K5 (from peg 5–9).
Knit 2 over 1 on peg 9.
Row 10: K6 (from peg 9–4).
Knit 2 over 1 on peg 4.
Row 11: K7 (from peg 4–10).
Knit 2 over 1 on peg 10.
Row 12: K8 (from peg 10–3).
Knit 2 over 1 on peg 3.
Row 13: K9 (from peg 3–11).
Knit 2 over 1 on peg 11.
Row 14: K10 (from peg 11–2).
Knit 2 over 1 on peg 2.
Row 15: K11 (from peg 2–12).
Knit 2 over 1 on peg 12.
Row 16: K12 (from peg 12–1).
Knit 2 over 1 on peg 1.

Working the Sock Foot

Note: The sock foot is worked in the round.
Rnd 1: K12, p1, k4, p2, k4, p1.
Next Rnds: Repeat rnd 1 until work measures 5cm (2in) less than desired length.

Shaping the Toe

Note: The toe is worked as a flat panel. The cup is formed by knitting short rows just like for the heel. Remember to wrap each of the turning pegs.

Row 1: K11 (from peg 1–11), W&T peg 12.
Row 2: K10 (from peg 11–2), W&T peg 1.
Row 3: K9 (from peg 2–10), W&T peg 11.
Row 4: K8 (from peg 10–3), W&T peg 2.

Row 5: K7 (from peg 3–9), W&T peg 10.
Row 6: K6 (from peg 9–4), W&T peg 3.
Row 7: K5 (from peg 4–8), W&T peg 9.
Row 8: K4 (from peg 8–5), W&T peg 4.
Row 9: K5 (from peg 5–9). Make sure to knit 2 over 1 on peg 9.
Row 10: K6 (from peg 9–4). Knit 2 over 1 on peg 4.
Row 11: K7 (from peg 4–10). Knit 2 over 1 on peg 10.
Row 12: K8 (from peg 10–3). Knit 2 over 1 on peg 3.
Row 13: K9 (from peg 3–11). Knit 2 over 1 on peg 11.
Row 14: K10 (from peg 11–2). Knit 2 over 1 on peg 2.
Row 15: k11 (from peg 2–12). Knit 2 over 1 on peg 12.
Row 16: k12 (from peg 12–1). Knit 2 over 1 on peg 1.

Closing the Toe and Finishing
In preparation for closing the toe, take the stitches off the knitting loom and place them onto a pair of 5mm (US size 8) knitting needles like this: Take the stitches from peg 1–12 and place them on 1 knitting needle. Take stitches from peg 13–24 and place them on a second knitting needle.

Graft the front and back stitches together (see page 50). Weave in all ends. Block lightly.

Mock Cable Socks

Socks that you can wear with everyday shoes are possible to loom knit; all you need is a loom that is fine enough to give you the desired tension. The pattern is knitted with a modified mock cable.

MATERIALS

Knitting Loom

68 peg extra fine gauge round loom

Yarn

366m (400yd) of fingering weight/sock weight yarn [Koigu Premium Merino, 100% merino wool, 160m (175yd) per 50g (1¾oz) used in sample]

Tools

Knitting tool
Tapestry needle
2 2.75mm (US size 2) double-pointed knitting needles

Size

Adult (foot length adjustable in pattern)

Tension

8 sts per 2.5cm (1in)

Pattern notes
Knitted in the round.

Abbreviations
RTW = twist right (take the loops off pegs A and B, place stitch from peg A on peg B, place stitch from peg B on peg A). Knit them.

Cable Twist Rib Pattern
Multiple of 4
Rnds 1, 2, 4: K1, p1, k2
Rnd 3: K1, p1, RTW

Stitch Pattern Chart

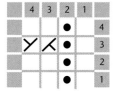

Key

☐	Knit
●	Purl
✕	Right Twist

Sock Leg

Note: Rounds 1–4 are the Cable Twist Rib pattern, a 4-stitch repeat.

Cast on in the round with Chain Cast On method (see page 43).
Rnd 1, 2, 4: K1, p1, k2
Rnd 3: K1, p1, RTW
Rep rounds 1–4 (Cable Twist Rib pattern) until item measures 16.5cm (6½in) from cast on edge (or desired length), ending with rnd 4 ready for short-row heel.

Working the Short-row Heel

The heel is worked as a flat panel. The cup for the heel is formed by knitting short rows. Remember to wrap each of the turning pegs. Knit heel as instructed in the short-row heel chart (right).

Working the Sock Foot

Knit the sole and instep areas of the sock in the round. Instep area will have mock cables, sole of foot will be in Stocking Stitch.

**Rnd 1, 2, 4: K34, [k1, p1, k2] 8 times, end with K2.
Rnd 3: K34, [k1, p1, RTW] 8 times, end with RTW**.
(Rounds 1–4: Knit 34, from peg 35–68 follow Mock Cable Stitch pattern instructions).

Next Rounds: Repeat from ** to ** until foot measures 5cm (2in) less than desired length.

Short Row Heel Chart

68 Peg Loom – 25.5cm (10in)

Part I: Decrease	Part II: Increase	
Knit from peg to peg	Wrap peg. These pegs will have 2 loops on them. Lift the loop on the peg, wrap the peg, place loop back on the peg.	Be sure to knit over 2 over 1 on the pegs with the extra loop on them.
1–34	35	13–24
34–2	1	24–12
2–33	34	12–25
33–3	2	25–11
3–32	33	11–26
32–4	3	26–10
4–31	32	10–27
31–5	4	27–9
5–30	31	9–28
30–6	5	28–8
6–29	30	8–29
29–7	6	29–7
7–28	29	7–30
28–8	7	30–6
8–27	28	6–31
27–9	8	31–5
9–26	27	5–32
26–10	9	32–4
10–25	26	4–33
25–11	10	33–3
11–24	25	3–34
24–12	11	34–2
12–23	24	2–35
23–13	12	35–1

Shaping the Toe

The toe is worked as a flat panel. The cup is formed by knitting short-rows as in the heel. Remember to wrap each of the turning pegs. Rep short row heel chart.

Closing the Toe

Take stitches from pegs 1–32 and place them on one double-pointed knitting needle. Take stitches from pegs 33–64 and place them on the second double-pointed knitting needle.

Graft the front and back stitches together (see page 50). Weave in all ends. Block lightly.

Weekend Socks

Spend your weekend mornings lounging around in style. These socks sport classic mock cables with a background of reverse stocking stitch.

Pattern notes

Adjust the suggested size by knitting more or fewer rounds in the leg and foot area.

Abbreviations

TW = twist right (take the loops off pegs A and B, place stitch from A on peg B, place stitch from peg B on peg A). Knit the two stitches.
W&T = wrap and turn. Remove loop from peg, E-Wrap peg, place loop back on the peg. Knit back in the opposite direction.

Stitch Pattern

Mock Cable Rib Pattern: 4-stitch repeat
Rnds 1, 2, 4: [P1, k2, p1] 6 times
Rnd 3: [P1, TW, p1] 6 times

Chart

4	3	2	1	
•	|	|	•	4
•	/	/	•	3
•	|	|	•	2
•	|	|	•	1

Chart Key
K Knit |
P Purl •
TW Twist /

Sock Leg

Cast on 24 sts and prepare to work in the round.
Note: Rounds 1–4 are the Mock Cable Rib Pattern

Rnd 1, 2, 4: [P1, k2, p1] 6 times.
Rnd 3: [P1, TW, p1] 6 times.

Rep rnds 1–4 (mock cable rib pattern) until leg measures 15cm (6in) from cast on edge or 7 Mock Cable Rib Pattern repetitions have been completed.
End sock leg with rnd 4.

Short-row Heel

Note: The heel is worked as a flat panel. The cup for the heel is formed by knitting short rows. Remember to wrap each of the turning pegs.

Row 1: K11 (from peg 1–11), W&T peg 12.
Row 2: K10 (from peg 11–2), W&T peg 1.
Row 3: K9 (from peg 2–10), W&T peg 11.
Row 4: K8 (from peg 10–3), W&T peg 2.
Row 5: K7 (from peg 3–9), W&T peg 10.
Row 6: K6 (from peg 9–4), W&T peg 3.
Row 7: K5 (from peg 4–8), W&T peg 9.
Row 8: K4 (from peg 8–5), W&T peg 4.

(continued on next page)

Row 9: K5 (from peg 5–9). Be sure to knit 2 over 1 on peg 9.
Row 10: K6 (from peg 9–4). Be sure to knit 2 over 1 on peg 4.
Row 11: K7 (from peg 4–10). Be sure to knit 2 over 1 on peg 10.
Row 12: K8 (from peg 10–3). Be sure to knit 2 over 1 on peg 3.
Row 13: K9 (from peg 3–11). Be sure to knit 2 over 1 on peg 11.
Row 14: K10 (from peg 11–2). Be sure to knit 2 over 1 on peg 2.
Row 15: K11 (from peg 2–12). Be sure to knit 2 over 1 on peg 12.
Row 16: K12 (from peg 12–1) Be sure to knit 2 over 1 on peg 1.

Sock Foot

The sock foot is worked in the round.

Rnds 1, 2, 4: k12, [p1, k2, p1] 3 times.
Rnd 3: k12, [p1, TW, p1] 3 times.

Next Rnds: rep rounds 1–4 until 5cm (2in) less than desired length.

Shape the Toe

The toe is worked as a flat panel. The cup is formed by knitting short rows just like above for the heel. Remember to wrap each of the turning pegs.

Row 1: K11 (from peg 1–11), W&T peg 12.
Row 2: K10 (from peg 11–2), W&T peg 1.
Row 3: K9 (from peg 2–10), W&T peg 11.
Row 4: K8 (from peg 10–3), W&T peg 2.
Row 5: K7 (from peg 3–9), W&T peg 10.
Row 6: K6 (from peg 9–4), W&T peg 3.
Row 7: K5 (from peg 4–8), W&T peg 9.
Row 8: K4 (from peg 8–5), W&T peg 4.
Row 9: K5 (from peg 5–9). Be sure to knit 2 over 1 on peg 9.
Row 10: K6 (from peg 9–4). Be sure to knit 2 over 1 on peg 4.

Row 11: K7 (from peg 4–10). Be sure to knit 2 over 1 on peg 10.
Row 12: K8 (from peg 10–3). Be sure to knit 2 over 1 on peg 3.
Row 13: K9 (from peg 3–11). Be sure to knit 2 over 1 on peg 11.
Row 14: K10 (from peg 11–2). Knit 2 over 1 on peg 2.
Row 15: K11 (from peg 2–12). Knit 2 over 1 on peg 12.
Row 16: K12 (from peg 12–1). Knit 2 over 1 on peg 1.

Closing the Toe and Finishing

In preparation for closing the toe, take stitches from peg 1–12 and place them on one knitting needle. Take stitches from peg 13–24 and place them on the second knitting needle.

Graft the front and back stitches together (see page 50). Weave in all ends. Block lightly.

Flat Panel Patterns

These are all knitted in flat panels or single rakes.
You don't need a special loom; you can use a circular
loom without joining the stitches up into a round.
Have fun!

Trendy Scarf

Grab a ball of some funky, novelty yarn and knit an extraordinary flat panel scarf. The Trendy Scarf knits up quickly on a large gauge knitting loom.

MATERIALS

Knitting Loom

12 peg large gauge loom

Yarn

82m (90yd) bulky weight novelty yarn [Jo-Ann Sensations Halo, 100% nylon, 45m (49yd) per 50g (1¾oz) ball used in sample]

Tools

Tapestry needle
Knitting tool

Size

10 x 112cm (4 x 44in)

Pattern notes
Worked completely as a flat panel. Selvedge Stitches slipped throughout

Abbreviations
k = Knit Stitch
p = Purl Stitch
sl1 = slip 1

Instructions
Cast on 12 stitches.
Row 1: Sl1, k11.
Row 2: Sl1, p11.
Repeat Rows 1–2 until item measures 76cm (30in).

Divide scarf for keyhole opening: Attach a second ball of yarn to the seventh peg.

Next row: Sl1, k5.
Pick up the new yarn attached to peg 7 and knit to peg 12.
Next row: Sl1, p5. Drop yarn and pick up the other skein of yarn and Purl to peg 12.
Repeat above 2 rows 3 times.
Rejoin the two sides. Remove one of the balls and work entire row with one strand.
Next row: Sl1, k11.
Next row: Sl1, p11.
Repeat Rows 1–2 until item measures 112cm (44in) from cast on edge.
Cast off with Basic Cast Off method (see page 36).

Urban Chic Cowl

Wear this chic cowl as a long scarf, or double it up for an urban chic look. The knitted fabric texture brings to life this luscious merino wool.

MATERIALS

Knitting Loom

26 peg large gauge loom.

Yarn

247m (270yd) super bulky merino wool [Malabrigo Rasta, 100% merino wool, 82m (90yd) per 150g (5¼oz) skein used in sample]

Tools

Knitting tool
Tapestry needle

Measurements

147 x 25cm (58 x 10in)

Tension

10 stitches and 16 rows to 10cm (4in) in pattern.

Pattern notes

Worked as a flat panel. Cast on edge and cast off edge are seamed together to create a circular item. Skip the first peg of the row with yarn behind the peg and knit the last peg.

Abbreviations

k = Knit Stitch
p = Purl Stitch
sts = stitches
sl = slip (skip the peg with the working yarn behind the peg)

Instructions

Cast on 26 sts, prepare to work a flat panel.

Row 1: Sl 1, *k1, p1; rep from * to last peg, k1.
Row 2: Sl 1, *p1, k1; rep from * to last peg, k1.
Row 3: Sl 1, *p1, k1; rep from * to last peg, k1.
Row 4: Sl 1, *k1, p1; rep from * to last peg, k1.
Rep Rows 1–4 until panel measures 147cm (58in) from cast on edge. Cast off with Basic Cast Off method (see page 36), leaving a 51cm (20in) yarn tail. Using a tapestry needle, sew the cast on edge to the cast-off edge. Weave ends in. Block lightly.

Garter Stitch Scarf

One simple design can be used for a quick, thin, fashionable scarf, or wider for a warm wrap. We knitted the thin style in the red yarn to match the Garter Stitch hat and fingerless gloves. For added pizazz, add some long tassels or a fringe.

MATERIALS

Knitting Loom

12 peg large gauge knitting loom

Yarn

Thin Scarf: 146m (160yd) super bulky weight yarn [Rowan Big Wool, 100% wool, 79m (87yd) per 100g (3½oz) ball in Bohemian]

Tools

Knitting tool

Size

183 x 15cm (72 x 6in)

Tension

8 stitches and 12 rows to 10cm (4in)

Pattern notes

Knitted as a flat panel.
Slip the first stitch at the beginning of each row.
The scarf was worked with the Knit Stitch. If you desire a more open weave, I recommend using Single Stitch instead (see page 31).

Abbreviations

k = Knit Stitch
p = Purl Stitch
sl1 = slip 1

Stitch pattern

Garter Stitch

Instructions

Cast on 12 stitches.

Row 1: Sl1, p 10, k1.
Row 2: Sl1, k to end.

Rep rows 1 and 2 until scarf measures 183cm (72in), or desired length.

Cast off using the Basic Cast Off method (see page 36). Weave in yarn ends.

 TIP

When adding another skein of yarn, add it at the beginning of a row. Make sure to leave at least a 12.5cm (5in) tail at the end of the old skein and on the beginning of the new skein. For a nice chain edge, slip the first stitch and knit the last stitch of each row.

Fingerless Mitts

These easy hand warmers can keep your hands toasty while allowing finger movement – perfect for those early mornings at the computer or knitting on a cold day. Knit them to match the cosy Garter Stitch hat and scarf.

MATERIALS

Knitting Loom

18 peg large gauge knitting loom

Yarn

46m (50yd) super bulky weight yarn [Rowan Big Wool, 100% wool, 79m (87yd) per 100g (3½oz) ball in Bohemian used in sample]

Tools

Knitting tool
Tapestry needle
Stitch marker

Size

Medium adult

Tension

8 stitches and 12 rows to 10cm (4in) in garter stitch

Pattern notes

Knitted as a flat panel

Abbreviations

k = Knit Stitch
p = Purl Stitch
Inc = increase

Instructions

Make 2.
Cast on 18 stitches with the Chain Cast On method (see page 43), leaving a beginning yarn tail of about 50cm (20in).
Rows 1 and 3: Purl.
Rows 2 and 4: Knit.
Rows 5–14: Knit.
Row 15: Inc 1 stitch at beginning of row. K 18 sts.
Row 16: Increase 1 stitch at beginning of row. K 19 sts. [20 sts]
Rows 17–26: Knit.

Row 27: p2, place an open ring stitch marker on the third stitch, p to end.
Row 28: Knit.
Row 29: Purl.
Cast off loosely using Basic Cast Off method (see page 36), leaving a 25.5cm (10in) yarn tail.

Assembly

Using the yarn tail end from the cast on edge and mattress stitch, seam the side of the mitt. Stop 4cm (1½in) from the row with the stitch marker. Secure and then cut yarn. Thread the tapestry needle through the yarn tail end on the cast off edge. Use Mattress Stitch to seam the side, stopping when you reach the row with the stitch marker. You should have an open section for your thumb to fit through. Weave the yarn ends into the wrong side of the item. Remove all stitch markers.

Cowl

The cowl is knitted with brushed alpaca yarn for a soft neck covering to keep out the chills. You can wear this cowl two ways – around your neck, or over your head – but whichever way you choose, wear it with style.

MATERIALS

Knitting Loom

40 peg large gauge knitting loom

Yarn

101m (110yd) of baby alpaca yarn [Plymouth Baby Alpaca Brush, 80% Baby Alpaca, 20% Acrylic, 101m (110yd) per 50g (1¾oz) used in sample]

Tools

Knitting tool
Tapestry needle

Size

56cm (22in) circumference, 36cm (14in) long

Tension

13 sts and 14 rows to 10cm (4in)

Pattern notes
Knitted as a flat panel.

Abbreviations
Sl = slip the stitch with yarn in the back
k = Knit Stitch
p = Purl Stitch

Instructions
Cast on 40 sts and prepare to work a flat panel.

Row 1: Sl1, k to the end.
Row 2: Sl1, p2, k to last 3 sts, p3.
Repeat rows 1 and 2 until item measures 56cm (22in) from cast on edge.

Cast off with Basic Cast Off method (see page 36).

Assembly
Seam the cast on edge to the cast off edge.
Block lightly.

Rainbow Fish Pillow

Learn the basics of increasing and decreasing on a flat panel by creating a cute bedroom pillow for a child.

MATERIALS

Knitting Loom

20 peg regular gauge loom

Yarn

92m (100yd) bulky weight yarn [1 ball Berroco Air, 78% Wool, 22% Nylon, 106m (115yd) per 50g (1¾oz) skein was used in sample]

Tools

Knitting tool
Tapestry needle

Other

Button for eye
Polyester batting for stuffing

Size

Approx. 30.5 x 12.5cm (12 x 5in)

Tension

10 stitches and 14 rows to 10cm (4in)

Pattern notes

Item is worked as a flat panel in Garter Stitch (alternating knit and Purl rows).

Abbreviations

k = Knit
p = Purl
Inc 1 = increase 1 stitch with Lifted Increase method (see page 57)
ssk = Slip, Slip, Knit
k2tog = knit 2 together

Instructions

Make 2
Cast on 20 stitches with Cable Cast On method (see page 42).
Row 1: Purl.
Row 2: K2, k2tog, k to last 4 sts, ssk, k2.
Row 3: Purl.
Row 4: Knit.
Rep Rows 1–4 until you have 6 stitches remaining.
Knit 2 rows of Garter Stitch.

Continue to increasing section
Row 1: Purl.
Row 2: K2, inc 1, k to last 2 sts, inc 1, k2.
Row 3: Purl.
Row 4: Knit.
Rep Rows 1–4 until 20 stitches are on the loom.
Knit 8 rows of Garter Stitch. You should have 16 Garter Stitch rows in total.

Continue to decreasing section
Row 1: P.
Row 2: K2, k2tog, k to last 4 sts, ssk, k2.
Row 3: P.
Row 4: K.
Rep Rows 1–4 until you have 6 sts remaining.
Knit 1 row of Garter Stitch.

Assembly

Fix a button to represent the eye using a tapestry needle and matching yarn. Sew and stuff the body of the fish.

Caution: If knitting this item for a very young baby, embroider an eye instead of attaching the button.

Brocade Baby Sweater

This baby sweater has a simple drop-shoulder and boatneck design. It is knitted with a non-itchy wool blend yarn that does not shed, which is great for baby projects.

MATERIALS

Knitting Loom

23 (27, 31) peg large gauge loom

Yarn

146, (165, 201) m (160 (180, 220) yd) bulky weight yarn [GGH Aspen, 50% fine merino wool, 50% Microfibre, 58 m (63 yd) per 50 g (1¾ oz) used in sample]

Tools

Knitting tool
Tapestry needle

Other

2 buttons

Size

Newborn (6 months, 12 months)

Tension

10 sts and 16 rows to 10 cm (4 in)

Pattern notes

Knitted as 4 flat panels.
The instructions are presented as follows: newborn (6 months, 12 months). Where only one number appears, the same instructions apply for all sizes. Always knit the first and last stitch of the row. They are Selvedge Stitches and are not part of the stitch pattern.

Abbreviations

k = Knit Stitch
p = Purl Stitch
St st = Stocking Stitch (knit every row)
M1 = Make 1 using the Lifted Increase method (see page 57)
CO = cast on

Stitch Pattern

Mini Brocade stitch
Multiple of 4+1 over 5 rows

Key

☐ **Knit** stitch
● **Purl** stitch

Pattern:

Row 1 (RS): k2, p, k2
Row 2: k, p, k, p, k
Row 3: p, k3, p
Row 4: k, p, k, p, k
Row 5: k2, p, k2

Back

Cast on 23 (27, 31) sts with the Chain Cast On method (see page 43).

Hemline

All sizes
Row 1: Knit.
Row 2: Purl.
Rep rows 1–2.
Size 12 months only, rep rows 1–2 once more.
Next 2 rows: All sizes work 2 rows in St st.

Mini Brocade Stitch Pattern

Row 1: K3, *p1, k3; rep from * to end.
Row 2: K2, *p1, k1; repeat from * to last 2 sts, k2.
Row 3: K1, p1, *k3, p1; rep from * to last st, k1.
Row 4: K2, p1, *k1, p1; rep from * to last 2 sts, k2.

Rep Rows 1–4: 8 (9, 10) more times, ending on a row 1.

Neckline

Knit 2 rows.
Cast off with Basic Cast Off method (see page 36).

Front

Follow instructions for back, stopping at neckline instructions.

Front Neckline

Next row: K6, (8, 9) BO 11 (11, 13), k6 (8, 9).

Divide neckline into two parts.
Each part has 6 (8, 9) pegs.
Next row: K6 (k8, k9).
Next row: K6 (k8, k9).

Make Buttonholes
Next row: K1 (k1, k2), k2tog, k1
(k2, k1), k2tog (k1, k2).
Next row: K2 (k2, k3), CO 1, k1
(k2, k1), CO 1, k1 (k2, k3).
Next row: K6 (k8, k9). Cast off. Join
yarn to the other side.
Next row: K6 (k8, k9). Cast off.

Sleeves
Make 2
Cast on 15 (19, 23) sts with
Chain Cast On method.

Cuff
All sizes
Row 1: Knit.
Row 2: Purl.

Rep rows 1–2.
Size 12 months only, rep rows 1–2
once more.
All sizes:
Next row: Knit.
Next row: K2, m1, k to last 2 sts,
m1, k2. [17 (21, 23) sts]
Next row: *K3, p1; rep from *
to the last st, p1.
Next row: K1, m1, p1, *k1, p1; rep
from * to last st, m1, k1. [19 (23,
27) sts]
Next row: K1, p1, *k3, p1; rep
from * to last st, k1.
Next row: K2, p1, *k1, p1; rep
from * to last 2 sts, k2.
Continue in Mini Brocade Pattern.
Row 1: K3, *p1, k3; rep from *
to end.
Row 2: K2, *p1, k1; rep from *
to last 2 sts, k2.
Row 3: K1, p1, *k3, p1; rep from *
to last st, k1.

Row 4: K2, p1, *k1, p1; rep from *
to last 2 sts, k2.
Rep these 4 rows 5 (6, 7) more
times.

Next row: Rep row 1 Brocade
pattern.
Next row: Knit.
Cast off. Block lightly.
Weave in all ends.

Assembly
Join front to back along right
shoulder. Pin front to back along
left shoulder where buttons will
go. Seam top of sleeves to main
sweater, aligning centre of sleeves
to shoulder seam. Join sleeve and
sweater sides. Unpin left shoulder
and attach 2 buttons to correspond
to buttonholes.

Newborn

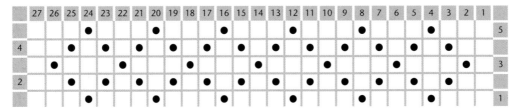

6 months

12 months

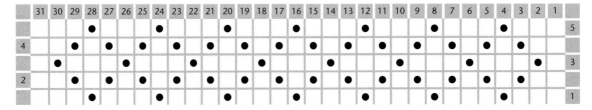

Velvety Soft Blanket and Hat

The name of this blanket and hat describes them perfectly. The yarn used for the project is next-to-the-skin worthy – perfect for a newborn baby. Knitted with a large gauge knitting loom this baby layette knits fast.

MATERIALS

Knitting Loom

For blanket: 40 peg large gauge knitting loom
For hat: 24 peg large gauge hat loom

Yarn

For blanket: 150m (165yd) bulky weight chenille yarn [Lion Brand Velvetspun, 100% Polyester, 49m (54yd) per 85g (3oz) skein used in sample: 2 skeins Carnation, 1 skein White]
For hat: 46m (50yd) bulky weight chenille Yarn [Lion Brand Velvetspun, 100% Polyester, 49m (54yd) per 85g (3oz) skein used in sample]

Tools

Knitting tool
Tapestry needle

Size

Blanket: 56 x 56cm (22 x 22 in)
Hat: Newborn–6 months

Tension

7 stitches and 15 rows to 10cm (4in) in pattern

Pattern notes (Blanket)

Knitted as a flat panel.
Main colour (MC) Carnation.
Contrasting colour (CC) White.

Pattern notes (Hat)

Knitted in the round.

Abbreviations

MC = main colour
CC = contrasting colour
ss = Single Stitch
p = Purl Stitch
sl1 = slip 1

Stitch Pattern:

E-Wrap Garter Stitch
Row 1: Sl1, p38, ss1.
Row 2: Sl1, ss to end.

Blanket Instructions

With MC, cast on 40 sts with the Chain Cast On method (see page 43).
Work in E-Wrap Garter Stitch for 26 rows. Cut MC leaving a 12.5cm (5in) tail. Join CC leaving a 12.5cm (5in) beginning tail. Work in E-Wrap Garter Stitch for another 26 rows. Cut CC leaving a 12.5cm (5in) tail. Attach MC leaving a 12.5cm (5in) beginning tail.
Work E-Wrap Garter Stitch pattern for 26 rows.

Cast off.
Weave in all yarn tail ends.

Hat Instructions

Using CC cast on 24 sts in the round

Hat

Rnd 1: Purl to end of rnd.
Rnd 2: Ss to end of rnd.
Rnd 3: P to end of rnd. Cut CC, leave a 12.5cm (5in) yarn tail.
Rnd 4: Join MC, ss to end of rnd.
Rnd 5: Ss to end of rnd.
Rep rnd 5 until item measures 12.5–15cm (5–6in) from cast on edge.
Cast off using Gather Cast Off method (see page 35). Weave in yarn tail ends.

TIP

Wrap loosely when knitting with chenille yarn. It breaks very easily! Be sure to bind in the ends well so it doesn't unravel.

Bliss Baby Blanket

This baby blanket is knitted in Debbie Bliss Cashmerino, an exquisitely soft, washable yarn. The yarn is gentle on the skin and it knits up fast on a large gauge knitting loom.

MATERIALS

Knitting Loom

38 peg large gauge knitting loom

Yarn

868m (950yd) of bulky weight yarn [Debbie Bliss Cashmerino Super Chunky, 55% merino wool, 33% microfibre, 12% cashmere, 76m (83yd) per 100g (3½oz) ball was used in sample]

Tools

Knitting tool
Tapestry needle
Crochet hook

Size

91 x 97cm (36 x 38in)

Tension

12 sts and 20 rows to 10cm (4in) in stocking stitch.
Make sure you check tension.

Pattern notes

Knitted as 3 flat panels.

Abbreviations

k = Knit Stitch
p = Purl Stitch
St st = Stocking Stitch
Rep = Repeat

Stitch Patterns

Moss Stitch (for even number of sts in row)
Row 1: *P1, k1; rep from * to end.
Rep Row 1

Stocking Stitch
Work every row in Knit Stitch.

Panel 1 (Make 1)

Cast on 38 stitches with chain cast on method (see page 43). The first and last stitches are Selvedge Stitches.

Row 1: k1, p1, to last st, k1
Rep row 1 until panel measures 30.5cm (12in) **.
Next Rows: work in St st for 30.5cm (12in).
Repeat from ** to **.
Cast off with Basic Cast Off method (see page 36).

Panel 2 (Make 2)

Cast on 38 stitches with Chain Cast On method.

The first and last stitches are Selvedge Stitches.
Row 1: K1, [p1, k1] to last st, k1
Rep row 1 until panel measures 91cm (36in).

Cast off with Basic Cast Off method.

Assembly

Block the pieces lightly prior to assembly.
Place panel 1 between the other two panels (see assembly diagram below). Use Mattress Stitch to seam the panels. Weave in all ends.
Once all the panels are assembled, Single Crochet all around the blanket to neaten the edges.

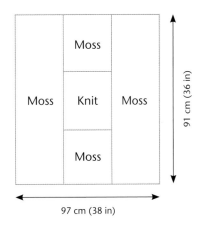

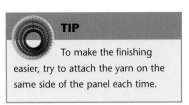

TIP

To make the finishing easier, try to attach the yarn on the same side of the panel each time.

Mock Cables Poncho

Ponchos are a classic garment – while remaining stylish at all times of course. An easy knit and versatile item of clothing, this poncho is knitted with a large gauge knitting loom and bulky yarn to grow quickly.

MATERIALS

Knitting Loom

22 (28, 36) peg large gauge knitting loom

Yarn

232 (290, 406) m / 256 (315, 441) yd of bulky weight yarn [GGH Aspen in Off White (50% fine merino wool, 50% microfibre, 58m (63yd) per 50g (1¾oz) used in sample]

Tools

Knitting tool
Tapestry needle

Sizes

Children 4 (6, 8) years (middle size shown in photograph). See also size chart on page 155 for adult sizes.

Tension

6 stitches and 8 rows to 5cm (2in) when blocked

Abbreviations

k = Knit Stitch
p = Purl Stitch
sl1 = slip 1
TW = twist (Mock Cable)

Stitch Pattern

Mock Cable
TW = twist
1 Twist right (take the loops off pegs A and B, place stitch from peg A on peg B, place stitch from peg B on peg A).
2 Knit the two stitches.

Stitch Pattern Chart

8	7	6	5	4	3	2	1	
4 •	•	|	|	•	•	|	|	
•	•	/	/	•	•	|	|	3
2 •	•	|	|	•	•	|	|	
•	•	|	|	•	•	|	|	1

Chart Key
K Knit |
P Purl •
TW Twist /

Panels (Make 2)
Note: The first and last stitch are Selvedge Stitches, they are not part of the stitch pattern.
Rows 1–4 are the Mock Sable Stitch pattern, an 8-stitch repeat.

Cast on 20 (28, 36) stitches with Chain Cast On method (see page 43).

Rows 1, 2, 4: Sl1, [k2, p2, k2, p2] 2, (3, 4) times, k3.
Row 3: Sl1, [k2, p2, TW, p2] 2, (3, 4) times, k3.

Work until panel measures 46 (53, 64) cm / 18 (21, 25) in or you have repeated rows 1–4, 18 (21, 25) times.

End by working a row 4.

Cast off with Basic Cast Off method (see page 36).

Block pieces to the following measurements:
25.5 (30, 36) x 53 (61, 74) cm (10 (12, 14) x 21 (24, 29) in)

Assembly
Assemble the poncho by seaming a long side to a short side. Fold over into poncho shape and seam a short side to a long side. See assembly diagram below.

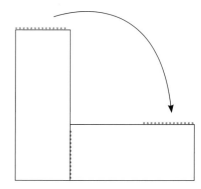

Ruana

This Ruana will provide you with warmth during those autumn days. It can be worn in different styles: let the front and back down, throw one or both of the front panels up around your shoulders – it's up to you!

MATERIALS

Knitting Loom

40 peg large gauge loom

Yarn

974m (1,066yd) bulky weight yarn [Debbie Bliss Cashmerino super chunky, 12% cashmere, 55% merino wool, 33% microfibre, 65m (71yd) per 50g (1¾oz) used in sample]

Tools

Knitting tool
Stitch markers

Size

76 x 142cm (30 x 56in)

Tension

12 stitches and 20 rows to 10cm (4in)

Pattern Note

Knitted in two panels.

Abbreviations

k = Knit Stitch
p = Purl Stitch
BO = cast off
RTW = twist right (take the loops off pegs A & B, place stitch from peg A on peg B, place stitch from peg B on peg A, knit both stitches)
LTW = twist left, mirror image of RTW

Border Edge Patterns

Mock Cable outside edge stitch pattern completed over 6 stitches
Left Side Panel
Row 1, 2, 3: P2, k2, p2.
Row 4: P2, RTW, p1.
Repeat Rows 1–4.

Chart 1: Mock Cable Edge

	6	5	4	3	2	1	
4	●	●	⅄	⅄	●	●	
	●	●			●	●	3
2	●	●			●	●	
	●	●			●	●	1

Legend:
☐ Knit
● Purl
⅄⅄ Right Twist

Chart 2: Moss Stitch

	4	3	2	1	
4		●		●	
	●		●		3
2		●		●	
	●		●		1

Legend:
☐ Knit
● Purl

Moss Stitch: inside edge stitch pattern – completed over 4 stitches.
Row 1: *K1, p1; rep from * to end.
Repeat row 1.

Part 1: Left Side Panel:

See chart 3: Left side panel (page 124)

Set up: Place stitch markers on pegs 3 and 4 to mark the Mock Cable Stitches. Place the remaining 4 stitch markers on the last 4 pegs (pegs 37–40). Cast on 40 sts using Chain Cast On method (see page 43).

Rows 1, 3: P2, k2, p2, k30, [k1, p1] twice.
Row 2: [K1, p1] twice, k30, p2, k2, p2.
Row 4: [K1, p1] twice, k30, p2, RTW, p2.
Rep rows 1–4, 25 times (25 cables).

Shaping the neckline (over 20 rows): the Moss Stitch is extended over 10 more stitches. The outside edge maintains the Mock Cable Stitch edge. (See Chart 5, page 124).
Rows 1, 3, 5: P2, k2, p2, k20, [k1, p1] 7 times.
Row 2: [K1, p1] 7 times, k20, p2, k2, p2.
Row 4: [K1, p1] 7 times, k20, p2, RTW, p2.

Neckline opening
Row 6: BO 10, [k1,p1] twice, k20, p2, k2, p2. (30 sts remain on loom.)
Row 7: P2, k2, p2, k20, [k1, p1] twice.

Row 8: [K1, p1] twice, k20, p2, RTW, p2.
Row 9: P2, k2, p2, k20, [k1, p1] twice.
Row 10: [K1, p1] twice, k20, p2, k2, p2.
Row 11: Rep row 9.
Row 12: Rep row 8.
Row 13: Rep row 9.
Row 14: Cast on 10 sts, rep row 10.
Row 15: P2, k2, p2, k20, [k1, p1] 7 times.
Row 16: [K1, p1] 7 times, k20, p2, RTW, p2.
Row 17: Rep row 15.
Row 18: [K1, p1] 7 times, k20, p2, k2, p2.
Row 19: Rep row 15.
Row 20: Rep row 16.
End of neckline shaping.

**Next row: P2, k2, p2, k34.
Next row: K34, p2, k2, p2.
Next row: P2, k2, p2, k34.
Next row: K34, p2, RTW, p2**.
Rep from ** to ** 24 more times (you should have 25 Mock Cables). Knit 6 rows of Moss Stitch. Cast off with Basic Cast Off method (see page 36).

Part 2: Right Side Panel:
See chart 4: Right side panel (page 124)
Place stitch markers on pegs 37 and 38 to mark the Mock Cable Stitches. Place the remaining 4 stitch markers on the first 4 pegs (pegs 1–4). Cast on 40 stitches using Chain Cast On method.

Rows 1, 3: [P1, k1] twice, k30, p2, k2, p2.
Row 2: P2, k2, p2, k30, [p1, k1] twice.
Row 4: P2, LTW, p2, k30, [p1, k1] twice.
Rep rows 1–4 24 more times – 25 cables on the edge.

Shaping the neckline (over 20 rows): the Moss Stitch is extended over 10 more stitches. The outside edge maintains the Mock Cable Stitch edge. (See Chart 6, page 125).

Rows 1, 3, 5: [P1, k1] 7 times, k20, p2, k2, p2.
Row 2: P2, k2, p2, k20, [p1, k1] 7 times.

Row 4: P2, LTW, p2, k20, [p1, k1] 7 times.

Neckline opening
Row 6: P2, k2, p2, k20, [p1, k1] twice, BO 10. (30 sts remain on loom).
Row 7: Join yarn by peg 12. [p1, k1] twice, k20, p2, k2, p2.
Row 8: P2, LTW, p2, k20, [p1, k1] twice
Row 9: [P1, k1] twice, k20, p2, k2, p2.
Row 10: P2, k2, p2, k20, [p1, k1] twice.
Row 11: [P1, k1] twice, k20, p2, k2, p2.
Row 12: P2, LTW, p2, k20, [p1, k1] twice.

Chart 3: Left Side Panel

40	39	38	37	36	35	34	33	32	31	30	29	28	27	26	25	24	23	22	21	20	19	18	17	16	15	14	13	12	11	10	9	8	7	6	5	4	3	2	1	
	●		●																															●	●	⌐	⌐	●	●	4
●		●																																●	●		●	●	3
	●		●																															●	●		●	●	2
●		●																																●	●		●	●	1

Legend:

☐ Knit

● Purl

⌐⌐ Right Twist

Notes: Left Side Panel

Chart 4: Right Side Panel

40	39	38	37	36	35	34	33	32	31	30	29	28	27	26	25	24	23	22	21	20	19	18	17	16	15	14	13	12	11	10	9	8	7	6	5	4	3	2	1	
●	●	⌐	⌐	●	●																															●		●		4
●	●			●	●																														●		●		3
●	●			●	●																													●		●			2
●	●			●	●																														●		●		1

Legend:

☐ Knit

● Purl

⌐⌐ Left Twist

Notes: Beginning of Right Side Panel

Chart 5: Left Side Neckline Shaping

Legend:

☐ Knit

● Purl

⌐⌐ Right Twist

✕ No Stitch

Row 13: [P1, k1] twice, k20, p2, k2, p2.

Row 14: P2, k2, p2, k20, [p1, k1] twice, CO 10.

Row 15: [P1, k1] twice, k20, p2, k2, p2 (40 stitches).

Row 16: P2, LTW, p2, k20, [p1, k1] 7 times.

Row 17: [P1, k1] 7 times, k20, p2, k2, p2.

Row 18: P2, k2, p2, k20, [p1, k1] 7 times.

Row 19: [P1, k1] 7 times, k20, p2, k2, p2.

Row 20: P2, LTW, p2, k20, [p1, k1] 7 times.

End of neckline shaping.

**Next row: K34, p2, k2, p2,

Next row: P2, k2, p2, k34

Next row: K34, p2, k2, p2

Next row: P2, LTW, p2, k34**

Rep from ** to ** 24 more times (you should have 25 Mock Cables).

Knit 6 rows of Moss Stitch.

Cast off with Basic Cast Off method.

Block panels lightly.

Part 3 Assembly

Place both panels right side up on a flat surface. Arrange the panels so they are mirror images of each other. The neckline opening should be a rectangle in the centre. The Mock Cables should be on the outside edge, while the Moss Stitch edge should be at the middle of the front side; the back side should have the Stocking Stitch edges against each other.

Seam the back side of the Ruana with Mattress Stitch (see page 51).

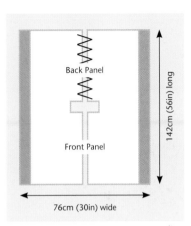

Back Panel
Front Panel
142cm (56in) long
76cm (30in) wide

Chart 6: Right Side Neckline Shaping

Row	40	39	38	37	36	35	34	33	32	31	30	29	28	27	26	25	24	23	22	21	20	19	18	17	16	15	14	13	12	11	10	9	8	7	6	5	4	3	2	1
24	●	●	✗	✗	●	●																					●		●		●		●		●		●		●	
23	●	●			●	●																						●		●		●		●		●		●		●
22	●	●			●	●																					●		●		●		●		●		●		●	
21	●	●			●	●																						●		●		●		●		●		●		●
20	●	●	✗	✗	●	●																					●		●		●		●		●		●		●	
19	●	●			●	●																						●		●		●		●		●		●		●
18	●	●			●	●																					●		●	X	X	X	X	X	X	X	X	X	X
17	●	●			●	●																						●		X	X	X	X	X	X	X	X	X	X
16	●	●	✗	✗	●	●																					●		●	X	X	X	X	X	X	X	X	X	X
15	●	●			●	●																						●		X	X	X	X	X	X	X	X	X	X
14	●	●			●	●																					●		●	X	X	X	X	X	X	X	X	X	X
13	●	●			●	●																						●		X	X	X	X	X	X	X	X	X	X
12	●	●	✗	✗	●	●																					●		●	X	X	X	X	X	X	X	X	X	X
11	●	●			●	●																						●		X	X	X	X	X	X	X	X	X	X
10	●	●			●	●																					●		●	X	X	X	X	X	X	X	X	X	X
9	●	●			●	●																						●		●		●		●		●		●		●
8	●	●	✗	✗	●	●																					●		●		●		●		●		●		●	
7	●	●			●	●																						●		●		●		●		●		●		●
6	●	●			●	●																					●		●		●		●		●		●		●	
5	●	●			●	●																						●		●		●		●		●		●		●
4	●	●	✗	✗	●	●																					●		●		●		●		●		●		●	
3	●	●			●	●																						●		●		●		●		●		●		●
2	●	●			●	●																					●		●		●		●		●		●		●	
1	●	●			●	●																						●		●		●		●		●		●		●

Legend:

☐ Knit

● Purl

✗✗ Right Twist

✗ No Stitch

Notes: Beginning of Right Side Panel

Waves Shrug

When you do not want to wear a sweater, or a shawl, the shrug comes to the rescue. The Waves Shrug is knitted with a simple Purl and Knit design that will remind you of small waves hitting the shore.

MATERIALS

Knitting Loom

60 peg regular gauge loom

Yarn

366m (400yd) of bulky weight yarn [Berroco Softwist, 59% rayon, 41% wool, 92m (100yd) per 50g (1¾oz) used in sample]

Notions

Knitting tool
Tapestry needle

Size

112 x 43cm (44 x 17in)

Tension

16 sts and 24 rows to 10cm (4in) in Stocking Stitch

Pattern Note

Item is knitted all in one flat panel. Knit extra/fewer stitch pattern repeats in the body of the shrug to make the shrug longer or shorter.

Abbreviations

k = Knit Stitch
M1 = Make 1 (creates an increase)
k2tog = knit 2 stitches together (creates a decrease)

Stitch Patterns

Rib Stitch Pattern

Multiple of 4 stitches
Row 1: *K2, p2; rep from * to end.
Row 2: *P2, k2; rep from * to end.

Legend:
☐ Knit   ● Purl

Wave Stitch Pattern

Multiple of 12 stitches
Row 1: P2, k7, p3.
Row 2: K2, p2, k5, p2, k1.
Row 3: K2, p2, k3, p2, k3.
Row 4: K4, p5, k3.
Row 5: Knit.
Row 6: Knit.

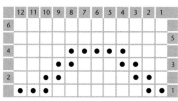

Legend:
☐ Knit   ● Purl

Cuff

Cast on 52 stitches with Chain Cast On method (see page 43)

**Row 1: *K2, p2; rep from * to end.
Row 2: *P2, k2; rep from * to end**
Repeat from ** to ** until cuff measures 20.5cm (8in) from cast on edge. End on a row 2.
Next row: K2, m1, k1, p2, *k2, p2; rep from * to last 2 sts, m1, p2. [54 sts]
Next row: P3, *k2, p2; rep from * to last 3 sts, k3.
Next row: K2, m1, k2, p2, *k2, p2; rep from * to last 5 sts; k2, p1, m1, p3. [56 sts]
Next row: P4, *k2, p2; rep from * to the last 4 sts; k4.
Next row: K2, m1, k3, p2, *k2, p2; rep from * to last 2 sts, m1, p3. [58 sts]
Next row: P5, *k2, p2; rep from * to last 5 sts; k5.
Next row: K2, m1, k4, p2, *k2, p2; rep from * to last 3 sts; p1, m1, p3. [60 sts]
Next row: Knit.

Body

Knitted in Wave Stitch Pattern.

***Row 1: *P2, k7, p3; rep from * to end.

Row 2: *K2, p2, k5, p2, k1; rep from * to end.

Row 3: *K2, p2, k3, p2, k3; rep from * to end.

Row 4: *K4, p5, k3; rep from * to end.

Row 5: Knit.

Row 6: Knit.***

Repeat from *** to *** until body area measures 72cm (28in) ending with a row 6.

Cuff

Next row: K2, k2tog, k2, p2, *k2, p2; rep from * to last 4 sts; p2, p2tog, p2. [58 sts]

Next row: P5, *k2, p2; rep from * to last 5 sts, k5.

Next row: K2, k2tog, k1, p2, *k2, p2; rep from * to last 7 sts, k2, p1, p2tog, p2. [56 sts]

Next row: P4, *k2, p2; rep from * to last 4 sts, k4.

Next row: K2, k2tog, p2, *k2, p2; rep from * to last 6 sts; k2, p2tog, p2. [54 sts]

Next row: P3, *k2, p2; rep from * to last 3 sts, k3.

Next row: K1, k2tog, p2, *k2, p2; rep from * to last 5 sts, k2, p2tog, p1. [52 sts]

**Next row: *P2, k2; rep from * to end.

Next row: *K2, p2; rep from * to end.**

Repeat from ** to ** until ribbing measures 20.5cm (8in).

Cast off with Basic Cast Off method (see page 36). Block lightly.

Assembly

Fold piece lengthwise. Mattress Stitch (see page 51) seam each cuff area plus 10cm (4in) or until you reach the desired place.

Glasses Case

This is a great project to try out a new stitch pattern. Here we have used Double Moss, or Seed Stitch, but any will do.

MATERIALS

Knitting Loom

18 peg large gauge knitting loom

Yarn

37m (40yd) of bulky weight yarn [Simply Soft Quick, 100% Acrylic, 46m (50yd) per 85g (3oz) skein used in sample]

Tools

Knitting tool
Tapestry needle

Size

14 x 7.5cm (5½ x 3in)

Tension

6 stitches and 10 rows to 5cm (2in) over Double Moss Stitch

Pattern notes

Knitted as a flat panel.

Abbreviations

k = Knit Stitch
p = Purl Stitch
k2tog = knit 2 stitches together

Stitch Pattern

Double Moss Stitch: multiple of 2 stitches.

Row 1: *K1, p1, repeat from * to the end of the row.

Row 2: *P1, k1, repeat from * to the end of the row.

Row 3: *P1, k1, repeat from * to the end of the row.

Row 4: *K1, p1, repeat from * to the end of the row.

Instructions

Cast on 18 stitches with the Chain Cast On method (see page 43). Knit in Double Moss Stitch pattern until item measures 16.5cm (6½in) from cast on edge.

Next row: Cast off 2 stitches. Knit 14. Cast off last 2 stitches. Cut yarn. Attach yarn to the fourteenth stitch. Continue knitting in Double Moss Stitch pattern for 4cm (1½in).

Next row: Continue workng in pattern as follows: work first 3 stitches in pattern. K2tog. Work in pattern to the last four stitches. K2tog. Work in pattern to end.

Next row: Repeat previous row.

Next rows: Work in pattern for another 2.5cm (1in). Cast off with the Basic Cast Off method (see page 36).

Assembly

Fold the glasses case in half. Mattress Stitch the short side seams. Attach two buttons so they match the buttonhole openings made by the k2tog.
Weave in all yarn ends.

Assembly diagram

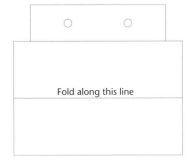

Fold along this line

Board patterns

Knitting on a straight board creates a much thicker knitted fabric than regular circular loom knitting. This is where the quality of loom knitting really comes into its own.

Power Pink Scarf

Hip scarf knitted with a fun novelty yarn. It is a quick knit on a large gauge knitting board. Knit it longer than necessary for a fashionable look.

MATERIALS

Knitting Loom

16 peg (8 from each side) regular gauge knitting board

Yarn

128m (140yd) of bulky weight novelty yarn [Patons Twister, 65% Polyester, 35% Acrylic, 43m (47yd) per 50g (1¾oz) skein used in sample]

Tools

Knitting tool
Tapestry needle

Size

173 x 10 (68 x 4in)

Tension

Not important

Pattern notes

Knitted completely with Figure 8 Stitch (see page 71), which allows for an Open Weave Stitch that permits the 'feathery' properties of the Twister yarn to fluff up.

Instructions

Cast on 8 sets of stitches (16 pegs total; 8 from each side).

Row 1: Work Figure 8 Stitch to end. Repeat row 1 until scarf reaches desired length.

Cast off loosely. Weave in ends.

Scarflet

A small project to learn decreases and increases on a knitting board. Use a special brooch to give this small scarflet a unique touch.

MATERIALS

Knitting Loom

24 peg (12 from each side) regular gauge knitting board

Yarn

60m (65yd) of bulky weight yarn [Berroco Pleasure, 66% Angora, 29% Merino Wool, 5% Nylon, 119m (130yd) per 50g (1¾oz) was used in sample]

Tools

Knitting tool
Crochet hook

Size

43 x 10cm (17 x 4in)

Tension

11 sts and 14 rows to 10cm (4in)

Pattern notes
Worked completely in Stocking Stitch (see page 70).

Abbreviations
k2tog = knit 2 together, creates a decrease (see page 75).

Instructions
Cast on 12 sets of stitches.

Knit for 36cm (14in) in Stocking Stitch.

**Decrease row: K1, k2tog, knit to last 3 sts, k2tog, k1.

Next two rows: Knit**.
Repeat from ** to ** 3 times.
[6 sets of sts on board]
Cast off.

Double Knit Ribbed Scarf

Alpaca yarn is perfect for this project – soft and cosy to keep you extra warm during the winter months. The ribbed structure allows the scarf to sit comfortably around the neck.

MATERIALS

Knitting Loom

24 peg (12 from each side) regular gauge knitting board

Yarn

110m (220yd) of super bulky weight yarn [Misti Alpaca Chunky, 99m (108yd) per 100g (3½oz) hank used in sample]

Notions

Knitting tool
Crochet hook

Size

193 x 12.5cm (76in x 5in)

Tension

11 sts and 14 rows to 10cm (4in)

Pattern notes
Worked entirely in Rib Stitch (see page 70).

Instructions
Cast on 12 sts.
Row 1: Work Rib Stitch to end.
Rep Row 1 for 193cm (76in)
Cast off. Block lightly.

Striped Scarf

Don't hide your true stripes. Use odds and ends of yarn that you have in your stash already to get creative. Experiment by varying the width of the stripes, or even make the stripes in a novelty yarn for extra fun.

MATERIALS

Knitting Loom

24 peg (12 from each side) regular gauge knitting board

Yarn

114m (125yd) MC, 46m (50yd) CC of super bulky weight yarn [Caron Simply Soft Quick, 100% acrylic, 46m (50yd) per 85g (3oz) skein used in sample]

Tools

Knitting tool
Crochet hook

Size

183 x 12.5cm (72 x 5in)

Tension

10 sts and 12 rows to 10cm (4in)

Pattern notes

Knit completely in Stocking Stitch (see page 70).

Abbreviations

MC = main colour
CC = contrasting colour

Instructions

Cast on 12 sets of pegs with MC.
Work 6 rows with MC. Join CC. Work 2 rows with CC. Cut CC, leave a 12.5cm (5in) tail.
Repeat from ** to ** until scarf measures 178cm (70in) from cast on edge.
Work 6 rows with MC.
Cast off.

TIP

When doing small stripes (1–3 rows) it is not necessary to cut the yarn. Carry the colours up the side, weaving in at the end of each

Rosy Berry Throw

Curl up with this cosy throw to read your favourite book. A variety of different stitches give it wonderful texture and it is bound to become a family heirloom.

MATERIALS

Knitting Loom

128 peg (64 from each side) regular gauge knitting board. Sample used the adjustable 71cm (28in) Knitting Board plus peg extenders, with mid spacing 2 cm (¾in)

Yarn

Approximately 1,509m (1,650yd) bulky weight merino wool blend [Knit Picks Biggo, 50% Superwash Merino Wool, 50% nylon, 101m (110yd) per 100g (3½oz) skein; 7 skeins #25622 Tea Green Heather (G), 8 skeins #25617 Carnelian Red (R) used in sample].

Tools

Knitting tool
Tapestry needle
Measuring tape
Crochet hooks, sizes 6mm and 5mm

Measurements

Approximately 96cm x 132cm (38in x 52in)

Tension

9 sts and 16 rows to 10cm (4in) in Stocking Stitch

Pattern note

Be sure to twist the balls of yarn at the colour changes so that the throw will be connected.

Abbreviations

k = Knit Stitch
p = Purl Stitch
St st = Stocking Stitch
sts = stitches
rep = repeat

Open Rib Stitch

Wrap the pegs in a St st. Then set up the Open Rib on the back board only. Do this by moving loop 2 to peg 1, loop 4 to peg 3, loop 6 to peg 5 and continue across all the stitches. The result is 2 loops on every other peg and the pegs between are empty. Every row will wrap only the pegs covered and regular wraps on front board. You will have 4 wraps on the pegs on the back board and the pegs between will remain empty. When you hook over, be sure to lift 2 loops over the top 2 loops. The front board will be the regular bottom loop over top loop.

Purl Stitch

This is accomplished when wrapping the peg. Place the working yarn below the loop on the peg. To work this stitch, use the smaller crochet hook, reach down through the original loop, and grab the new bottom loop. Bring it out and lift the loop on the crochet hook so that the loop on the peg is lifted

off. Place the loop on the crochet hook back onto the peg for the new stitch. Do this to each peg that you want the Purl Stitch to be.

Instructions

Centre

Cast on 64 sts using (G), St st. Purl Stitch: Alternate 1 Knit and 1 Purl across the loom.
Row 1: P1, k1 to end.
Row 2: K1, p1 to end.
Continue alternating these 2 rows for a total of 5 rows. Do this pattern on one side of loom. The other side can be all Knit Stitches.
Tie on (R) yarn. Cut and knot (G) yarn.
Work 4 rows of St st. Cut and knot the (R) yarn.
Tie on (G) yarn. Begin the Purl Stitch and work for 16 rows.

Section A

Work in (G) yarn with continuing Purl Stitch for 8 sts. At stitch 9, tie on (R) yarn and tie colours together. Complete the circular with the (G) yarn. Lay the (G) yarn aside. Change to Open Rib Stitch set up on centre 48 pegs. Work in Open Rib Stitch for these 48 stitches. Tie on second ball of (G) yarn and tie colours together. Work last 8 sts in Purl Stitch. Return the circular on the Purl Stitches and the (R) Open Rib Stitches. Hook over all, being careful to do the alternating Purl Stitch. Work section as set for total of 20 rows.

Section B

This section will repeat the first two-colour section except the Open Rib will be replaced with St st. You will work this section for 16 rows. Repeat Section A and Section B. End with section A so that you have 4 sections of A and 3 sections of B.

Working the opposite edge of throw

Cut and tie the (R) yarn.
Work the (G) yarn, continuing the Purl Stitch all across the loom.
Do this for another 16 rows.
Change to (R) yarn. Tie and knot the (G) yarn.
Work in St st for 4 rows.
Change to (G) yarn. Tie and knot the (R) yarn.
Work in Purl Stitch for a total of 5 rows. Cut yarn.
Cast off all sts with 2-Loop method and loose hand. Knot securely with last loop. Pull in any yarn tails with crochet hook.

Side panels of 2-colour stripes (knit 2)

Alternate the colours for the borders, working (G) in Purl Stitch on one side and St st on the other, and (R) in St st on both sides. Start by casting on 10 sts in (G) yarn with Purl Stitch. Work 5 rows.
Tie on (R) yarn. Leave the (G) yarn attached and just carry it through the red section. Repeat with the red yarn and carry it through the green section.
Now, continue working in St st and Purl Stitch as described above, with 4 rows of each colour, until you have 44 stripes completed. The 45th stripe (G) should be 5 rows.
Cast off at anchor yarn and on loom using 2-Loop method.

Finishing the Throw:

Once the two strips of stripe pieces are complete, you are ready to attach them to your throw. Place them out on a flat surface beside the centre of the throw. Secure the strips to the centre with some T-pins so that the sewing stays even (toothpicks work as well). Sew the strips matching the first two stripes with the centre stripes. Work the rest of it between, so that it all lies well. Sew with large tapestry needle and (G) yarn using invisible stitch. Be sure to keep the Purl sides together so that one side of the throw has Purl on all (G) sections, and the other side is all Knit Stitch. If you chose to do both sides with Purl design, good for you – that will be beautiful.

Tuck in any yarn tails remaining.

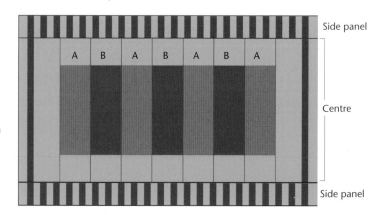

Felting Patterns

When natural fibres interlock with each other, they create a dense, strong fabric that is not prone to stretching. This means felting is ideally suited to items that get a lot of wear, like bags and slippers.

Yoga Mat Bag

Learn the basics of felting with this easy yet useful project. Choose a fun yarn to create a unique-to-you bag. Don't do yoga? It's okay, knit it anyway and use it to store your expanding knitting loom collection.

MATERIALS

Knitting Loom

36 peg large gauge loom

Yarn

274m (300yd) bulky weight wool [Manos del Uruguay, 100% wool, 125m (137yd) per 100g (3½oz) was used in sample]

Tools

Knitting tool
Tapestry needle

Other

Yoga mat for blocking purposes

Size

81 x 21.5cm (32 x 8.5in) (non-felted)
61 x 15cm (24 x 6in) (felted)

Tension

8 sts and 10 rows to 10cm (4in) (before felting)

Stitch Pattern

Garter Stitch
Rnd 1: Purl
Rnd 2: Knit
Rep rnds 1 and 2.

Instructions
Bag

Cast on in the round with Cable Cast On method (see page 42). Work in Garter Stitch until item is 81cm (32in) long. Cast off with Gather Cast Off method (see page 35).

Strap (Worked as flat panel)
Cast on 12 sts with Cable Cast On method.
Work in Garter Stitch until item is 91cm (36in) long. Cast off with Basic Cast Off method (see page 36).

Assembly

Attach strap to open rim (secure tightly). Attach strap to the bottom of the bag, place it about 8cm (3in) away from the centre of gathering removal. Felt (see page 24). To block, insert yoga mat inside and allow to air dry.

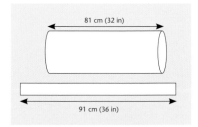

Felted Accessories Clutch

A small purse to carry all your essential loomy tools. This small clutch takes only a small amount of yarn and, knitted on a large gauge knitting loom, can be made in a jiffy.

MATERIALS

Knitting Loom

26 peg large gauge loom

Yarn

50m (55yd) bulky weight yarn [Lion Brand Landscapes, 50% wool, 50% Acrylic, 50m (55yd) per 50g (1¾oz) skein used in sample]

Other

25.5cm (10in) zip
Sewing needle
Matching thread

Tools

Knitting tool
Tapestry needle

Size

28 x 26.5cm (11 x 10.5in) (non-felted)
23 x 25.5cm (9 x 10in) (felted)

Tension

9.5 sts and 16 rows to 10cm (4in) (before felting)

Pattern notes

Worked as a flat panel.

Garter Stitch:

Row 1: Knit.
Row 2: Purl.
Rep Rows 1 and 2.

Instructions

Cast on 26 stitches with Chain Cast On method (see page 43).

Work in Garter Stitch, until panel measures 26.5cm (10½in) from Cast On edge.

Cast off with Basic Cast Off method (see page 36).

Assembly

Fold in half and seam along the two sides. Felt (see page 24). When dry, attach zip to opening with a sewing needle and matching thread.

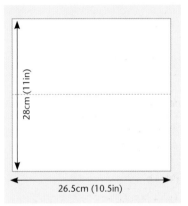

28cm (11in)

26.5cm (10.5in)

Felted Handbag

With its subtle grey and green stripes, this felted tote is perfect for everyday use, and will complement most outfits. The bag is completed on a round, large gauge knitting loom with at least 50 pegs, which is ideal for projects of this size.

MATERIALS

Knitting Loom

50 peg large gauge loom

Yarn

229m (250yd) bulky weight wool in colour A; 114m (125yd) bulky weight wool in colour B, 114m (125yd) bulky weight wool in colour C. [Brown Sheep, Lamb's Pride Bulky, 85% wool, 15% mohair 114m (125yd) per 100g (3½oz) was used in sample]

Tools

Knitting tool
Tapestry needle
Spool

Size

36 x 27cm (14 x 10½in)

Tension

12 sts and 16 rows to 10cm (4in) (before felting)

Pattern notes

Worked in Garter Stitch.

Garter Stitch:

Row 1: Knit.
Row 2: Purl.
Rep rows 1 and 2.

Tote Side 1

With colour A, cast on 50 sts with Cable Cast On method (see page 42).
Rows 1–16: Work in Garter Stitch. Cut colour A, leaving a 15cm (6in) yarn tail. Attach colour B.
Rows 17–26: Work in Garter Stitch. Cut colour B, leaving a 15cm (6in) tail. Attach colour C.
Rows 27–30: Work in Garter Stitch. Cut colour C, leaving a 15cm (6in) tail. Attach colour B.
Rows 31–32: Work in Garter Stitch. Cut colour B, leaving a 15cm (6in) tail. Attach colour C.
Rows 33–36: Work in Garter Stitch. Cut colour C, leaving a 15cm (6in) tail. Attach colour B.
Rows 37–46: Work in Garter Stitch. Cut colour B, leaving a 15cm (6in) tail. Attach colour A.
Rows 47–62: Work in Garter Stitch. Cast off 8 stitches each side. [34 stitches on the loom]

Tote Base

Using the 34 stitches that remain on the loom, work 32 rows in Garter Stitch.

Tote Side 2

Cast on 8 stitches on each side. [50 stitches]
Rows 1–62: Work in Garter Stitch, changing colour in the sequence used from side 1 in reverse order. Cast off with the Basic Cast Off method (see page 36).

Handles

Make two, 3-peg I-cords (see page 39), 51cm (20in) long.

Assembly

Seam the tote panels at the sides to form the tote. Felt the tote and the handles (see page 24).
Attach the handles as follows: Hold the two sides of the tote together and, with a tapestry needle, poke a hole through both panels, about 5cm (2in) from the top edges and 15cm (6in) from one seam. Pass the needle through both holes. Repeat 15cm (6in) from the other seam. Pass one I-cord through the two holes on one panel, and form a knot at each end inside the tote. Repeat on the other panel.

Felted Laptop Cosy

This super-easy bag is a great way to keep your laptop scratch free. The felted properties make it ideal for a laptop cosy as it will help keep moisture away in case of an accident.

MATERIALS

Knitting Loom

41 peg large gauge knitting loom

Yarn

293m (320yd) of super bulky weight wool [Rowan Big Wool, 100% wool, 80m (87yd) per 100g (3½oz), was used in sample]

Tools

Knitting tool
Tapestry needle

Tension

Pre-felted: 12 sts and 16 rows to 10cm (4in)

Size

Pre-felted:
41 x 41cm (16 x 16in)

Felted:
33 x 33 x 5cm
(13 x 13 x 2in)

Pattern Note

Slip the first stitch on every row. Knitted as a flat panel.

Abbreviations

k = Knit Stitch
p = Purl Stitch
Sl = Slip Stitch
BO = cast off
CO = cast on
St st = Stocking Stitch
MC = main colour
CC = contrasting colour

Instructions

Cast on 41 sts using E-Wrap Cast On method (see page 30) with MC.
Row 1: Knit.
Rep row 1 until piece measures 9cm (3½in).
Next row: Sl1, k13, BO13, k14.
Next row: Sl1, k13, CO13, k14.
Work in St st for 25.5cm (10in).
Cut MC. Join CC.
Work in St st for 5cm (2in).
Next row: Purl.
Next row: Knit.
Next row: Purl.
Work in St st for 5cm (2in).
Cut CC. Join MC.
Work in St st for 25.5cm (10in).

Next row: Sl1, k13, BO13, k14.
Next row: Sl1, k13, CO13, k14.
Work in St st for 9cm (3½in).
Cast off all stitches with Basic Cast Off method (see page 36).

Fold in half. Seam the sides.
Felt (see page 24).

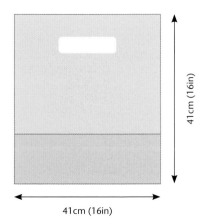

41cm (16in)

41cm (16in)

Soft Felt Slippers

I remember my feet dangling down from the chair with a pair of big red comfy slippers that my Grandma had knitted for me. The slippers in this pattern are a slide-on style – a quick knit and a perfect last-minute gift.

MATERIALS

Knitting Loom

31 peg large gauge loom

Yarn

110m (120yd) bulky weight non-superwash wool [Brown Sheep Lamb's Pride Bulky, 85% Wool, 15% Mohair, 114m (125yd) per 100g (3½oz) skein was used in sample]

Tools

Knitting tool
Tapestry needle
2 stitch markers
2 double-pointed knitting needles
Small pieces of suede for underside
Fabric glue or strong thread and needle for attaching suede soles

Tension

8 sts and 10 rows to 10cm (4in)

Size

Women's sizes 4 (5, 6)

Pattern notes

Worked flat and in the round.
Important: Add suede bottoms so the soles don't slip.

Abbreviations

CO = cast on
k = Knit Stitch
p = Purl Stitch
St st = Stocking Stitch
W&T = wrap and turn. Lift the loop off the peg, hold it with tool. E-Wrap peg, replace loop back on peg. Turn and knit in the other direction.
KO = knit over
KO 2/1 = knit the bottom 2 loops over and off the peg.

Instructions

Make 2
Place stitch markers on pegs 1 and 16. Cast on 16 stitches using E-Wrap Cast On method (see page 30) and proceed to make the heel as follows:
Row 1: k from peg 1–15; W&T peg 16.
Row 2: K from peg 15–2; W&T peg 1.
Row 3: K from peg 2–14; W&T 15.
Row 4: K from peg 14–3; W&T 2.
Row 5: K from peg 3–13; W&T 14.
Row 6: K from peg 13–4; W&T 3.
Row 7: K from peg 4–12; W&T 13.
Row 8: K from peg 12–5; W&T 4.
Row 9: K from peg 5–11; W&T 12.
Row 10: K from peg 11–6; W&T 5.
Row 11: K from peg 6–12; KO 2/1 on peg 12.
Row 12: K from peg 12–5; KO 2/1 on peg 5.
Row 13: K from peg 5–13; KO 2/1 on peg 13.

Row 14: K from peg 13–4; KO 2/1 on peg 4.
Row 15: K from peg 4–14; KO 2/1 on peg 14.
Row 16: K from peg 14–3; KO 2/1 on peg 3.
Row 17: K from peg 3–15; KO 2/1 on peg 15.
Row 18: K from peg 15–2; KO 2/1 on peg 2.
Row 19: K from peg 2–16; KO 2/1 on peg 16.
Row 20: K from peg 16–1; KO 2/1 on peg 1.**
Work 18 (20, 22) rows in St st.
Next row: k16, CO 15. [31 sts]
Begin knitting in the round.
Work 14 (16, 18) rounds in St st

Toe

Next rows: Work from ** to **.
Remove stitches from the loom onto two knitting needles:
Place sts 1–16 on one needle.
Place sts 17–31 on second needle.
Seam the toe using the Grafting method (see page 50).

Top bumper instructions

Make 2
Cast on 3 sts. Knit a 38 (41, 43) cm (15 (16, 17) in) length I-cord.

Assembly

Attach I-cord to top of slipper: start right below the instep area of the slipper and continue towards the heel and end on the other side. Felt (see page 24). Add suede soles with appropriate glue or stitching.

Stitch Patterns

Try out some of these stitch patterns on your projects to add different textures.

CHEVRON STITCH
Flat
(multiple of 8+1 sts; 4-row repeat)
Row 1: P1, k3, p1, k3, p1.
Row 2: K1, p1, k5, p1, k1.
Row 3: K2, p1, k3, p1, k2.
Row 4: K3, p1, k1, p1, k3.
Rep rows 1-4.

Circular
(multiple of 8 sts; 4-row repeat)
Round 1: P1, k3, p1, k3.
Round 2: K1, p1, k5, p1.
Round 3: K2, p1, k3, p1, k1.
Round 4: K3, p1, k1, p1, k2.
Rep Rounds 1-4.

BABY BASKET STITCH
Flat
(Multiple of 6+3 sts; 4-row repeat)
Row 1 and Row 2: *K3, p3; rep from * to last 3 sts, k3.
Row 3 and Row 4: *P3, k3; rep from * to last 3 sts, p3.

Circular
(Multiple of 6 sts; 4-row repeat)
Round 1 and Round 2: *K3, p3; rep from *.
Round 3 and Round 4: *K3, k3; rep from *.

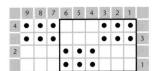

Legend:

☐ **Knit**
RS: Knit Stitch
WS: Purl Stitch

● **Purl**
RS: Purl Stitch
WS: Knit Stitch

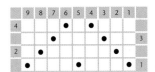

Legend:

☐ **Knit**   ● **Purl**

SEEDED COLUMNS
Flat
(multiple of 3 sts + 2; 2-row repeat)

Row 1: K to end.
Row 2: K2, *p1, k2; rep from * to end.
Rep rows 1 and 2.

Circular
(multiple of 3 sts; 2-row repeat)
Round 1: K to end.
Round 2: *K2, p1; rep from * to end.
Rep rounds 1 and 2.

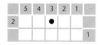

Legend:
☐ Knit ● Purl

DIAGONAL SEED STITCH
Flat
(multiple of 5 sts; 10-row repeat)
Row 1: *K4, p1; rep from *.
Row 2: *K1, p1, k3; rep from *.
Row 3: *K2, p1, k2; rep from *.
Row 4: *K3, p1, k1; rep from *.
Row 5: *P1, k4; rep from *.
Row 6: *P1, k4; rep from *.
Row 7: *K3, p1, k1; rep from *.
Row 8: *K2, p1, k2; rep from *.
Row 9: *K1, p1, k3; rep from *.
Row 10: *K4, p1; rep from *.
Rep rows 1–10.

Circular
(multiple of 5 sts; 5-row repeat)
Round 1: *K4, p1; rep from *.
Round 2: *K3, p1, k1; rep from *.
Round 3: *K2, p1, k2; rep from *.
Round 4: *K1, p1, k3; rep from *.
Round 5: *P1, k4; rep from *.
Rep rounds 1–5.

Legend:
☐ Knit ● Purl

MOSS STITCH
Flat
(multiple of 2+1 st; 2-row repeat)
Row 1: *P1, k1; rep from * to last st, p1.
Row 2: *K1, p1; rep from * to last st, k1.

Circular
(multiple of 2 sts; 2-round repeat)
Round 1: *P1, k1; rep from *.
Round 2: *K1, p1; rep from *.

Legend:

☐ **Knit**
RS: Knit Stitch
WS: Purl Stitch

● **Purl**
RS: Purl Stitch
WS: Knit Stitch

DOUBLE MOSS STITCH
Flat
(multiple of 2+1 st; 4-row repeat)
Row 1 and Row 2: *K1, p1; rep from * to last st, k1.
Row 3 and Row 4: *P1, k1; rep from * to last st, p1.

Circular
(multiple of 2 sts; 4-round repeat)
Round 1 and Round 2: *K1, p1; rep from *.
Round 3 and Round 4: *P1, k1; rep from *.

Legend:

☐ **Knit**
RS: Knit Stitch
WS: Purl Stitch

● **Purl**
RS: Purl Stitch
WS: Knit Stitch

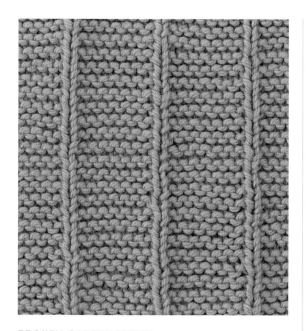

BROKEN GARTER STITCH
Flat
(Multiple of 8+7 sts; 1-row repeat)
Row 1: *P7, k1; rep from * to last 7 sts, p7.

Circular
(Multiple of 8 sts; 1-round repeat)
Round 1: *P7, k1; rep from *.

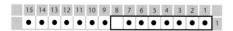

Legend:

☐ **Knit**
RS: Knit Stitch
WS: purl stitch

● **Purl**
RS: Purl Stitch
WS: Knit Stitch

GARTER PATTERN
Flat
(Multiple of 8+3 sts; 4-row repeat)

Row 1: *P3, k5; rep from * to last 3 sts, p3.
Row 2: P to end of row.
Row 3: *P3, k5; rep from * to last 3 sts, p3.
Row 4: P to end of row.

Circular
(Multiple of 8 sts; 4-round repeat)

Round 1: *P3, k5; rep from *.
Round 2: P to end of round.
Round 3: *P3, k5; rep from *
Round 4: P to end of round.

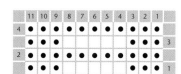

Legend:

☐ **Knit**
RS: Knit Stitch
WS: Purl Stitch

● **Purl**
RS: Purl Stitch
WS: Knit Stitch

	13	12	11	10	9	8	7	6	5	4	3	2	1	
8	●				●	●	●	●	●				●	
	●				●	●	●	●	●				●	7
6	●				●	●	●	●	●				●	
														5
4	●	●	●	●	●	●				●	●	●	●	
	●	●	●	●	●	●				●	●	●	●	3
2	●	●	●	●	●	●				●	●	●	●	
														1

Legend:

☐ **Knit** ● **Purl**

BASKET WEAVE

Flat
(multiple of 8+5 sts; 8-row repeat)
Row 1: *K13; rep from *.
Row 2: *P5, k3, p5; rep from *.
Row 3: *P5, k3, p5; rep from *.
Row 4: *P5, k3, p5; rep from *.
Row 5: *K13; rep from *.
Row 6: *P1, k3, p5, k3, p1; rep from *.
Row 7: *P1, k3, p5, k3, p1; rep from *.
Row 8: *P1, k3, p5, k3, p1; rep from *.

Circular
(multiple of 8 sts; 8-round repeat)
Round 1: *K8; rep from *.
Round 2: *P5, k3; rep from *.
Round 3: *P5, k3; rep from *.
Round 4: *P5, k3; rep from *.
Round 5: *K8; rep from *.
Round 6: *P1, k3, p4; rep from *.
Round 7: *P1, k3, p4; rep from *.
Round 8: *P1, k3, p4; rep from *.

Legend:
☐ Knit   ● Purl

GARTER STITCH ZIGZAG
Flat
(multiple of 6 sts; 12-row repeat)
Row 1: *K6; rep from *.
Row 2: *P3, k3; rep from *.
Row 3: *K6; rep from *.
Row 4: *P2, k3, p1; rep from *.
Row 5: *K6; rep from *.
Row 6: *P1, k3, p2; rep from *.
Row 7: *K6; rep from *.
Row 8: *K3, p3; rep from *.
Row 9: *K6; rep from *.
Row 10: *P1, k3, p2; rep from *.
Row 11: *K6; rep from *.
Row 12: *P2, k3, p1; rep from *.
Rep rows 1–12.

Circular
(multiple of 6 sts; 12-row repeat)
Round 1: *K6; rep from *.
Round 2: *K3, p3; rep from *.
Round 3: *K6; rep from *.
Round 4: *P1, k3, p2; rep from *.
Round 5: *K6; rep from *.
Round 6: *P2, k3, p1; rep from *.
Round 7: *K6; rep from *.
Round 8: *P3, k3; rep from *.
Round 9: *K6; rep from *.
Round 10: *P2, k3, p1; rep from *.
Round 11: *K6; rep from *.
Round 12: *P1, k3, p2; rep from *.
Rep rounds 1–12.

Glossary

Anchor Peg
The side peg on a knitting loom. Some knitting looms have a peg or thumb tack at the base of the loom. The anchor peg can be used to anchor the yarn.

Anchor Yarn
The yarn that is wrapped around the anchor peg on the knitting loom.

Ball of Yarn
A round bundle of yarn.

Basic Cast Off
The Basic Cast Off method is the method used to remove items off the knitting loom.

Beginning Tail End
The beginning yarn end found before the slip knot.

Block
The process of laying the knitted pieces flat on a surface, wetting them and giving them their shape.

Cast Off
Removing the item off the knitting loom. Knitting the very last row.

Cast Off in Pattern
Cast off the stitches as they are: Knit the Knit Stitches, Purl the purl Stitches as you cast them off the knitting loom.

Cast On Row
The first row on the knitting loom.

Casting On
The process of setting up the very first row. It becomes the foundation row of your knitted item.

Chunky Braid Stitch
A variation of the Single Stitch. Loom must have 4 loops on each peg to start knitting the Chunky Braid Stitch. Take yarn towards the inside of the knitting loom, wrap around the peg in a anticlockwise direction. Lift the bottommost 3 strands off the peg.

Double-Sided Frame
See Knitting Board.

Double-Sided Rake
See Knitting Board.

Double Stitch
A variation of the Single Stitch. Loom must have 2 loops on each peg to start knitting the Double Stitch. Take yarn towards the inside of the knitting loom, wrap around the peg in a anticlockwise direction. Lift the bottommost strand off the peg.

E-Wrap
It is the method by which we wrap a peg to form the Twisted Knit Stitch.

Fashion Stitch
Used on a knitting board, the Fashion Stitch provides an open weave.

Figure 8 Stitch
Used on a knitting board. It provides an open weave, recommended for novelty yarns.

Flat Removal Method
See Basic Cast Off.

Flat Stitch
See Knit Stitch.

Frog
Removing an item off the knitting loom as a result of a mistake.

Garter Stitch
Formed by combining a row of knits and a row of purls. Perfect for items that need to lay flat.

Gather Removal Method
The method used to close the top of a hat.

Tension
Also known as knitting gauge, this is the number of stitches and rows per inch. The size of each stitch varies depending on the yarn, knitting loom gauge, and loom knitter's tension.

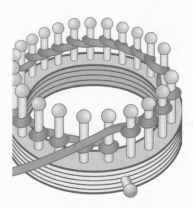

Graft
Join two edges together in an invisible way.

Knit Stitch
One of the foundation stitches. The Knit Stitch is done by placing the working yarn above the loop on the peg, inserting your knitting tool from the bottom up through the loop on the peg and catching the working yarn. Pull the working yarn through the loop on the peg. Remove the loop off the peg and place the newly formed loop on the peg.

Knitting Board
A double-sided rake. It creates a double-sided fabric that has no wrong side.

Knitting Loom
A general term that is used to refer to all types of looms, that is: circular, knitting frames, single-sided rakes.

Knitting Over (KO)
The process of forming a stitch. To knit over, you need to lift off one (or more) of the loops on the peg and let it fall off towards the centre of the knitting loom.

Loom Gauge
It refers to the measurement from peg to peg. Usually measured from centre of one peg to the centre of the next adjacent peg. Loom gauges range from extra fine 4mm (⅛in) to extra large gauge 2cm (¾in).

Lifeline
If you have a dropped stitch, place a line of stitching, or a stitch holder in the row below to stop it running.

Purl Stitch
One of the foundation stitches. The Purl Stitch is done by placing the working yarn below the loop on the peg, insert your knitting tool from the top down through the loop on the peg, catch the working yarn. Pull the working yarn through the loop on the peg. Remove the loop off the peg and place the newly formed loop on the peg.

Reverse Stocking
The bumpy side of a knitted fabric, formed by purling every single row.

Rib Stitch
A stitch that is formed by combining knits and purls.

Ribbing
See Rib Stitch.

Seaming
The process of joining two pieces of knitted fabric together.

Short Row
A technique used in shaping, it adds rows to a segment of the knitted piece. Used in loom knitting for shaping the heel and toe section.

Single-Sided Rake
A row of pegs that is used to make flat panels. A circular knitting loom can be used as a single-sided rake. A double-sided rake/knitting board can also be used as a single-sided rake by simply using only one side.

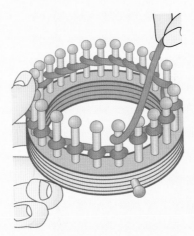

Single Stitch
The Single Stitch is done by wrapping around the peg in the E-Wrap method. Loom must have one loop on each peg to start knitting the Single Stitch. Take yarn towards the inside of the knitting loom, wrap around the peg in a anticlockwise direction. Lift the bottommost strand off the peg.

Slip Knot
It is a knot that is placed on the first peg. It becomes the first stitch.

Slip Stitch
Slipping a stitch on a knitting loom is done by simply skipping the peg. To slip the stitch, simply skip the peg with the yarn behind the peg.

Stocking
The smooth side of a knitted fabric. It resembles small Vs. Formed by knitting the Knit Stitch or Twisted Knit Stitch every single row.

Swatch
A piece of knitted fabric that is used to determine tension / gauge.

Tail End
The yarn that remains at the end of your knitted project.

Thread Loom
The process of casting on the very first row. See Cast On.

Tink
The word KNIT spelled backwards. It is done when you have made a mistake a few stitches back and you simply un-knit the stitches.

Twisted Knit Stitch
See Single Stitch.

Weave in Ends
When the knitted item is completed, you need to hide all the yarn tail ends. You weave the yarn tail ends into the wrong side of the item.

Working Yarn
The yarn coming from the yarn skein that is being used to knit on the knitting loom.

Yarn Tails
The lengths of yarn attached to a project before the first stitch and after the final stitch. Weave in once the project is finished.

U Stitch
Looks like a Knit Stitch, but is shorter in height. Hug the peg with the working yarn around the peg, then lift the bottommost loop up and off the peg.

Useful Information

Reading Charts

Charts are pictorial representations of stitch patterns, colour patterns, or shaping patterns.

Reading charts in loom knitting differs from reading a chart when needle knitting. In needle knitting, the knitting is turned after every row, exposing the wrong and right side of the fabric every other row. In loom knitting, the right side of the fabric is always in front, so we follow the pictorial chart as it appears.

- Charts are visual and pictorial representations of the stitch pattern. A chart allows you to see the entire stitch pattern.
- Charts are numbered on both sides, even numbers on the left side, odd on the right.
- Start reading the chart from the bottom.
- Each square represents a stitch.
- Each horizontal row of squares represents a row.
- Stitch pattern charts use symbols to represent stitches such as Knit, Purl, Twists, Yarn-Overs, and any other stitch manipulation needed.
- Thick black lines represent the end of a pattern stitch repeat. The stitches after the black line are Edge, or Selvedge Stitches.
- Charts for colour knitting differ from stitch pattern charts. In colour pattern charts each different colour square represents the colour needed for that particular stitch.

- For circular knitting: read the chart from bottom up from right to left.
- For flat knitting: read the chart from bottom up from right to left on odd rows, and from left to right on even rows.
- Remember: the right side of the knitted fabric is always facing the outside. Knit the stitches as they appear on the chart.

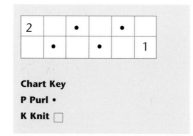

Chart Key
P Purl •
K Knit ☐

Chart reads:

For Flat Knitting:
Row 1: K1, p1, k1, p1.
Row 2: K1, p1, k1, p1.

For Circular Knitting:
Round 1: *K1, p1, rep from * to the end.
Round 2: *P1, k1, rep from * to the end.

A complete list of chart symbols and abbreviations used in this book is provided on the opposite page (we are using needle knitting standard abbreviations and symbols whenever possible).

Washing your Knits

Hand washing is the best washing technique for all your knitted items. Even those items that were knitted with machine washable yarns can have their life extended by practicing good washing habits.

Use pure soap flakes or special wool soap. Wash and rinse your item gently in warm water. Maintain an even water temperature; changing water temperature can shock your wool items and accidentally felt them. Before washing, test for colourfastness. If the yarn bleeds, wash the item in cold water. If the yarn is colourfast, wash with warm water.

Fill a basin or sink with water, add the soap flakes or wool soap, using your hands, gently wash the knitted item. Avoid rubbing, unless you want the yarn to mat and felt together.

To rinse, empty the basin and fill with clean warm water, immerse your knitted item and gently squeeze out all the soapsuds. Repeat until all the suds are gone and the water is soap free. Pat as much of the water out as you can using the palms of your hands. Do not wring your item as this may cause wrinkles and distort the yarn. Place the knitted item between two towels and squeeze as much of the water out as you can.

To dry your item, lay it flat somewhere away from direct sunlight. Block again, if necessary, to measurements.

Head Size Chart for Hats

Once you have got the hang of making hats you will want to design your own, or convert the patterns here to your own ends. Use this chart as a guide only to the average head sizes to help you.

	Size	Circumference	Depth
Preemie	Preemie 0.45–0.9kg (1–2lbs)	23–25.5cm (9–10in)	9–10cm (3.5–4in)
	Preemie 0.9–1.4kg (2–3lbs)	25.5–28cm (10–11in)	10cm (4in)
	Preemie 1.8–2.3kg (4–5lbs)	28–30cm (11–12in)	10cm (4in)
	Preemie 2.3–2.7kg (5–6lbs)	30–33cm (12–13in)	12.5cm (5in)
Baby	Newborn	33–36cm (13–14in)	12.5–15cm (5–6in)
	Baby 3–6 months	36–41cm (14–16in)	15–18cm (6–7in)
	Baby 6–12 months	41–48cm (16–19in)	18cm (7in)
Children	Toddler	46–51cm (18–20in)	20.5cm (8in)
	Child	48–51cm (19–20in)	20.5cm (8in)
Young Adults	Teens	51–56cm (20–22in)	23–25.5cm (9–10in)
Adults	Adult Woman	53–58cm (21–23in)	25.5cm (10in)
	Adult Man	56–61cm (22–24in)	25.5cm (10in)

Hats need to be loom knitted with a 2.5cm (1in) negative ease for a close fit, that is the hat should be slightly smaller when measured flat than the head it is to fit.

Poncho Conversion Chart

The lovely poncho pattern that we have supplied is designed for a small child. However, you can use the pattern provided here and adapt it to your own measurements. Use the table below to find the exact size of panels you need to make for your desired poncho size; then you can make one for every member of the family.

	Size	Panel Size Length	Panel Size Width
Baby/Toddler Size	12 Months	33cm (13in)	16.5cm (6.5in)
	2 Years	48cm (19in)	24cm (9.5in)
	4 Years	53cm (21in)	26.5cm (10.5in)
Child Sizes	6 Years	56cm (22in)	28cm (11in)
	8 Years	58cm (23in)	29cm (11.5in)
	10 Years	64cm (25in)	32cm (12.5in)
	12 Years	69cm (27in)	34.5cm (13.5in)
	14 Years	71cm (28in)	35.5cm (14in)
	16 Years	74cm (29in)	37cm (14.5in)
Woman's Size	X-small	71cm (28in)	35.5cm (14in)
	Small	74cm (29in)	37cm (14.5in)
	Medium	79cm (31in)	39.5cm (15.5in)
	Large	80cm (31.5in)	40cm (15.75in)
	1X	82cm (32in)	41cm (16in)
	2X	84cm (33in)	42cm (16.5in)
	3X–4X	86cm (34in)	43cm (17in)
	5X	88cm (34.5in)	44cm (17.25in)

Common Abbreviations Found in Loom Knitting

[ ]	work instructions in brackets as many times as directed
( )	work instructions in parentheses in the place directed
* *	repeat instructions between the asterisks as directed
*	repeat instructions following the single asterisk as directed
alt	alternate
approx	approximately
beg	begin/beginning
bet/btw	between
BO	cast off / bind off
but	buttonhole
CA	colour a
CAB	Cable
CB	colour b
cbs	Chunky Braid Stitch
CC	contrasting colour
CDD	centred double decrease from 3 sts down to 1. It is over 3 pegs, pegs are numbered as follows: peg 3 (left), peg 2, peg 1 (right). Move st from peg 1 to peg 2. Take working yarn behind peg 1 and peg 2, knit peg 3. Move st from peg 3 over to peg 2. Lift bottommost two stitches (loops) up and off the peg.
ch	chain (use a crochet hook)
cm	centimetres
cn	cable needle
co	cast on
col	colour
cont	continue
cr l	cross left
cr r	cross right
dbl	double
dec	decrease
diam	diameter
ds	Double Stitch

ew	E-Wrap
foll	follow/following
fc	front cross
fs	Flat Stitch/Knit Stitch
g	denotes grams
g st	Garter Stitch
hh	half hitch. Used to increase at the beginning of a new row. On the left side: with working yarn coming from the loom, make a loop (clockwise) so that the working yarn ends on the top. Flip it and place on the empty peg. The working yarn will be coming from underneath the loop and be ready to go to the right.
hs	Half Stitch
inc	increase
K or k	knit
kbl	knit through back of loop. In looming this is created by E-Wrap
KO	Knit Over
k2tog	knit 2 together – creates a right slanting decrease.
l	left
lc	left cross
lp(s)	loop (s)
LTW	left twist
m	denotes metres
M1	Make One. The M1 is an invisible increase st worked with a left or right slant. The right slant is used on the left side of the loom and vice versa. To prevent a hole forming, this increase st is twisted. To create the M1, move the st(s) outwards to open a peg for the new st. Reach for the bar coming from between the two sts, twist the bar anticlockwise (to create a right slant increase), or twist it clockwise (to create a left slanting increase), place it on the empty peg. On the

	following row/round, work the st as normal.
MC	main colour
mm	denotes millimetres
mul	multiple
oz	denotes ounces
P or p	Purl
p2tog	Purl 2 sts together – a right slanting decrease
pm	place marker
prev	previous
psso	pass slipped stitch over
rc	right cross
rem	remaining/remain
rep	repeat
rev St st	reverse stocking stitch
rnd(s)	round(s)
RS	right side
RTW	right twist
sc	single crochet
sel	selvedge
sk	skip
skn	skein
skp	Slip, Knit, pass stitch over – creates a decrease
sl	Slip
sl st	Slip Stitch
ss	Single Stitch
ssk	Slip, Slip, Knit these two stitches together – creates a left slanting decrease
ssp	Slip, Slip, Purl these two stitches together – creates a left slanting decrease
st(s)	stitch(es)
St st	Stocking Stitch (knit every row)
tog	together
tw	twist sts for a mock cable
W&T	wrap and turn
yds	yards
yo	yarn over

Suppliers

Knitting Looms

A variety of knitting looms were used in the making of the projects in this book. Visit your local craft store or do an internet search to source them.

Authentic Knitting Board
60 Carysbrook Road
Fork Union, VA 23055
www.knittingboard.com

Yarns

Berroco, Inc.
14 Elmdale Rd.
PO Box 367
Uxbridge, MA 01569
info@berroco.com
www.berroco.com

Brown Sheep Yarn Company
10062 County Road 16
Mitchell, NE 69357

Crystal Palace Yarns
160 23rd St
Richmond, CA 94804
www.straw.com

Joann.com
2361 Rosecrans Ave
El Segundo, CA 90245

Knitting Fever, Inc.
PO Box 502
Roosevelt, NY 11575
www.knittingfever.com

Koigu Wool Designs
RR #1
Williamsford, ON N0H 2V0
Canada
info@koigu.com

Lion Brand Yarns
135 Kero Road
Carlstadt, NJ 07072
www.lionbrand.com

Manos del Uruguay
www.rosiesyarncellar.com

Misti Alpaca
PO Box 2532
Glen Ellyn, Illinois, 60138
www.mistialpaca.com

Muench Yarns
285 Bel Marin Keys Blvd
Unit J
Novata, CA 94949
www.muenchyarns.com

Patons
PO Box 40
Listowel, ON N4W 3H3
Canada
www.patonsyarns.com

Plymouth Yarn Co.
PO Box 28
Bristol, PA 19007
pyc@plymouthyarn.com
www.plymouthyarn.com

Westminster Fibres
4 Townsend West
Nashua, NH 03063
www.rowan.com

Dedication

To my favourite people in the world: my husband Samuel and children, Bryant and Nyah. Thank you for your love, patience, and encouragement in my loom knitting endeavours.

Publisher's Acknowledgements

Thank you to Paul Forrester for photography, and the patient models: Jenny Doubt, Chris Lockwood, Bara Plevova, and Victoria Wiggins, plus Matilda Doran Jumaili, Alyssa Deacon, Ethan Deacon, Lois Durows, Lucy Grant, and Connor O'Neil. Thanks also to parents Maz Al-Jumaili, Nicola Deacon, Lisa Durows and Jane Laing.

Index

Bold page numbers denote projects.

Author's Acknowledgements

Thanks go first to all my friends in the loom knitting community – I would not have been able to write this book without your encouragement, input and support. Our love for loom knitting has given birth to this book. Loom on!

Special thanks to:
My editors Katy Bevan, Ruth Patrick, and Katy Denny for their encouragement, keen eye and creative advice. Anthony Duke, for the most outstanding artwork ever seen in loom knitting.

Thanks also to KB Looms and Provo Craft for providing us with knitting looms for photography.

My loom knitting friends and cheerleaders: Tina Edgar, for encouraging me to write the book and supporting me through the process in more ways than I can ever say; Becky Hansen, for her encouragement and technical support; Lori Lemiux, for introducing me to the world of felting; and to my non-loomy friends: Miriam Felton and Kimberly Petersen, for believing in me and cheering me on.